THE TABERNACLE

ITS STRUCTURE AND SYMBOLISM

Walter Scott

THIS EDITION
Published by

AMBASSADOR PRODUCTIONS LTD.
Providence House
Belfast BT5 6JR
Northern Ireland

ISBN 0 907927 26 2

FOREWORD

The Tabernacle: What A Glorious Subject! If anyone doubts its importance to the unveiling of God's ultimate Redemptive purposes in Christ, let that person consider the fact that the record of the creation occupies but two chapters of Holy Scripture, whereas details of the construction of the Tabernacle extends to fourteen chapters! The reason for this is plain: "The high and lofty One that inhabiteth eternity, whose name is Holy" (Isa. 57:15), had *walked* in Eden; he had *visited* Abraham, Isaac and Jacob; but now he desired *to dwell among* His People; and conditions for His Residence had to be right! Hence the fourfold charge to Moses: "See that thou make it according to the pattern I showed thee" ((Exodus 25:9, 40; 26:30 & 27:8).

Walter Scott: What A Gifted Scholar! Many have sought to expound the Treasures of Tabernacle Truth, but discerning readers can detect that not a few later authors have drawn liberal handfuls of their work from Walter Scott. In this reprinted volume we are privileged to be led in our study by the gracious saint himself. Some consider this to be Scott's greatest work, excelling even his "Exposition Of The Revelation."

Ambassador Publications: What A Great Service! In these days of widespread apostasy, when several publishing houses which once served the Lord's People by producing edifying titles have either had to close or diversify to meet frivolous demands of the times, it is refreshing to find one which is striving to reverse the popular trend, by being loyal to "The Old Paths." We salute Ambassador for their courage and enterprise.

Jack Mitchell,
Holywood,
Co Down, N. Ireland.
July 1988.

INTRODUCTION

The Tabernacle was an object lesson to Israel for nearly five hundred years — from Moses to David. It then gave place to the Temple, the more permanent structure. But the continuity of the great and blessed fact for Israel, namely the presence of Jehovah in the midst, is witnessed in the interesting circumstance that the *only* Tabernacle vessel transferred from the Tabernacle to the Temple was the Ark of the Covenant and its blood-sprinkled Mercy-seat — the recognised centre *within,* as the Brazen Altar was *without.*

Imperfectly at the best, and slowly, the faith of some — perhaps of many — looked beyond those dim outlines and faith shadows to God's revelation of *one* — foreshadowed by the Tabernacle in its wondrous structure, its mysterious veils, colours, and coverings, and its equally inexplicable sacrifices and ritual. The Law was the Jewish schoolmaster. The faith of the Christian rests on a fuller revelation and on the descent of the Holy Ghost — the Teacher and Guide of the Church. Our horizon is heaven and earth, and our faith comprehends the past and future, or from eternity to eternity, and thus exceeds by far that of the most advanced believer of Old Testament times.

The Tabernacle and all pertaining to it had a Divine meaning. The terms, "patterns" and "shadows," find their substance. Type, shadow, prediction, and prophecy converge in Christ. *One* Name, *one* Sacrifice, *one* Altar, *one* Sanctuary, and *one* High Priest in the heavens is God's answer and explanation of the Levitical system of old. Christ is all to God and all to us. What a galaxy of office and glory centres in Him!

The earnest prayer of the author is that *every* reader of the following pages may find therein abundant refreshment which may promote communion with God and His beloved Son — to whom be eternal glory!

Walter Scott,
Nottingham,
England.

CONTENTS.

——✳——

vi.   CONTENTS.—*Continued.*

CONTENTS.—*Continued*.

✳ ✳ ✳ ✳ ✳

THE TABERNACLE:

ITS STRUCTURE, VESSELS, COVERINGS, SACRIFICES, AND SERVICES.

~~~~~~~

The Tabernacle : God's Dwelling Place.

"LET them make Me a sanctuary, that I may dwell among them" (Exod. xxv. 8). The redemption of Israel by the might of Jehovah from the slavery and hard bondage of Egypt* was an accomplished and joyous fact (Exod. xiv.). It formed the great burden of that first and grand song recorded in history (xv.)—one exceeded only by the yet grander theme celebrated by the redeemed in the courts of heaven (Rev. v.).

Jehovah of old walked in Eden and held intercourse with Adam. He visited the patriarchs—the fathers of the nation. But He never had a home on earth till the Tabernacle was erected in the midst of His redeemed and happy people. Jehovah might have built a house for Himself—a palace befitting His glory and august presence. But no, He would have the *willing* hearted to give, and the *wise* hearted

---

* The blood of the Paschal Lamb sprinkled on the door posts and lintels of Israel's dwellings screened them from divine judgment, but that is not termed redemption. The blood kept God outside, for He was passing through Egypt on a mission of judgment. Redemption broke the power of the enemy, and set the people free for God and His service. This was effected at the Red Sea: see Exod. xiv. 13 ; xv. 13 ; Ps. cvi. 9, 10. Israel was redeemed by *power*, and is yet to be redeemed by *blood*. On the contrary, we are now redeemed by blood, and await redemption by power.

to build His house. It would be a labour of love on the part of all who gave or wrought. What a touching thought that each redeemed Israelite could have a part in building a sanctuary for Jehovah to dwell in. What rich and wondrous grace on the part of Jehovah to permit His people to build Him a house wherein He would dwell in their very midst, and inhabit their praises (Ps. xxii. 3). Seraph, cherub, and angel would have esteemed it a favour of the highest order to have had committed to them such a delightful service. But no, the hearts and hands of His redeemed are alone employed: "Let *them* make Me a sanctuary, that I may dwell among them." Besides the typical teachings and lessons of the Tabernacle—and these are rich and redolent of Christ—the first and primary use to which it was set apart was a dwelling for Jehovah—the Redeemer of Israel.

CONSTRUCTED BY DIVINE COMMAND.

The whole work, in its design and execution was *of God*. The Tabernacle and all that pertained to it, even to the pins, cords, and taches were planned and designed by the Spirit of God (Exod. xxxi. 3-6), Who 15 centuries afterwards comments upon His own workmanship (Heb. ix. 8). Not only was the pattern of the Tabernacle shewn to Moses, but the most minute and full instructions were given by God, so that not even the smallest detail, as colour, size, or material, was left to human imagination or wisdom. All was according to Divine command. Jehovah was the Architect of His own house. There are three chapters, in all of 98 verses, containing full and precise instructions for the erection of the Tabernacle (Exod. xxv., xxvi., xxvii.), and three chapters, also of 98 verses, shewing how fully and faithfully these Divine instructions were carried out to the very letter (xxxvi., xxxvii., xxxviii.) — three chapters of *command* answered by three chapters of *obedience*.

CONSTRUCTED FROM A DIVINE PATTERN.

The Tabernacle was not only constructed by Divine command, but also according to a Divine plan shewn to Moses on the mount (Exod. xxv. 9, 40; xxvi. 30). "According to all that I shew thee, the pattern of the Tabernacle and the pattern of all the instruments thereof, even so shall ye make it." The Tabernacle was the figure of things in the *heavens*. The Tabernacle was duly built according to the pattern shewn to Moses. He alone saw it; not even Aaron beheld it. "See, saith He, that thou make all things according to the pattern shewed to *thee* on the mount" (Heb. viii. 5); hence the pattern was the type, and the Tabernacle and its vessels the anti-type.

The Tabernacle and its sacred vessels were patterns or copies of things in the heavens (Heb. ix. 23, 24). In no sense did the Tabernacle typify the Church—the house of God—but rather bore testimony to Christ who tabernacled among us (John i. 14). Christ was the Tabernacle in which God dwelt. From chapter xxv. to xxvii. 19 the main thought is God revealing Himself to man, but inasmuch as "the only begotten Son which is in the bosom of the Father, He hath declared Him" (John i. 19)—so the Tabernacle in all its parts, especially in the portion pointed out, tells the story of Christ, the Revealer of God, His Divine and human natures; also His personal and official glories and offices. "God was in Christ."

The Tabernacle uttered one name, that name of priceless worth. Every whit of it expressed His glory, and were divinely intended to teach Christ, to shadow forth His sacrifice, His priesthood on high, His glories and beauties in the heavenly sanctuary, also to illustrate various relationships between God and His heavenly and earthly peoples. The Tabernacle also in its various parts figured the whole scene of creation, save the infernal regions.

The Court had its place in the world—the wide domain of Christian outward privilege, morally apart from the world, and set apart for those who would profit by these privileges. Thus the word of Jehovah was here spoken and heard by the assembled people; the Altar, Laver, etc., were also for use in the Court and in the presence of the people. The world proper was the wilderness outside the Court. The Court was *a* holy place (Lev. vi. 16).

Then the first part of the Tabernacle or holy place, was divided from the " holiest " by the beautiful veil rent at the death of Christ, and from the " Court " by the hangings or door at its entrance. Herein rested the Incense or Golden Altar, the Gold-Covered Table of Shewbread, and Seven-branched Golden Candlestick. It was in this holy apartment where the priests daily worshipped and served, which represents the heavenly places, the scene of the Church's blessing; *there* as worshippers we burn the fragrant incense in the presence of our God—the merits of Christ's Person and accomplished sacrifice; there, too, the Holy Spirit exhibits the varied glories of Christ as the lamps shone upon the beautifully carved shaft of the Candlestick, displaying its beauties; and there, too, we feed upon Christ as the priests did upon the Shewbread.

Next the second apartment or the "holiest," into which
the high priest alone entered once a year, and then to make
atonement. This was the most sacred spot on earth.
He entered with incense and blood, shadowing Christ in
His precious Person and infinite sacrifice. This apartment
directs us to the immediate presence of God. Now, just as
the high priest of old passed through the Court, and trod
the whole length of the Tabernacle till he stood with incense
and blood before the Mercy-seat, so Christ, our Great High
Priest, has gone from the Altar of divine judgment—the cross
really—and passed through the heavens in the value of His
Person and sacrifice, till He reached the throne at the right
hand of which He sits. To this Heb. iv. 14 refers: "Seeing
then that we have a great High Priest that is passed *through*
(not into) the heavens."

The Tabernacle and all connected with it was to be an
exact likeness of what was shewn to the Mediator. All
figured heavenly realities. The boards, colours, materials,
action, and services in the Court and in the Tabernacle—
without and within—are utterly senseless, and but a piece
of mere ritual unless Christ is brought in. He lights them
all up with meaning; He clothes these shadows with
substance—all have their answer in Him. The Altar and
the Ark—at the extreme, east and west of the Sacred
building—and all lying between, have absolutely no
significance unless as they throw their glory on Christ—
on what He *is* and on what He *does*. The Tabernacle
on earth was pitched by man; the true Tabernacle
in the heavens is pitched by the Lord (Heb. viii. 2).
The holy places on earth were the figures of the true
(Heb. ix. 23, 24). The heavenly things were to be

purified by the blood of Christ, not *beings* but *things*;
this cleansing is rendered necessary because of angelic
sin in the heavens (Ezek. xxviii.; Eph. vi.). The heavens
have been defiled, for Satan and fallen angels are there,
and hence the places needed cleansing. On the other hand,
the Tabernacle framed after the heavenly model, was
purified by the blood of sacrificial animals (Heb. ix. 21-24).
The heavens and earth need purification.

The Tabernacle in Hebrews ix. and Its Main Design.

The Tabernacle and its continual services for about 500
years was a silent yet eloquent teacher to Israel. It has
also been a fruitful source of study to the devout and
spiritual in all ages. The misty and dim apprehensions
of the people of old, have given place to a reverent understanding of Tabernacle teaching, for God has put into our
hands the key to unlock its meaning. The Epistle to the
Hebrews, especially chapters viii.-x., is the key. Christian
reader, take it up and use it for your souls' joy and profit.
Our studies in this delightful subject may be greatly
helped by careful attention to three expressions employed
in chapter ix.: (1) "The Tabernacle" referring to the
structure as a whole (first clause of verse 2). (2) "The
first Tabernacle" or holy place, the scene of constant
service and worship, figuring the whole Jewish system
which was characterised by continual doing and unfinished
service, and which necessarily kept man at a distance from
God. The veil unrent shut out God from man. The veil

rent is God's opened way for believers to enter His presence in boldness (Heb. x. 19). The veil was not removed, but sufficiently rent for any one to pass through and enter in in all the simplicity of faith (verses 6-9). (3) The "second" Tabernacle or "the holiest" within the veil, and into which the high priest could alone and only once yearly enter. The ineffable majesty and glory of Jehovah was centred in the holiest which figured the immediate presence of God—the Heaven of heavens. There, too, He dwelt between the cherubim, and from thence He governed the world.

THE MAIN DESIGN OF THE TABERNACLE.

The Tabernacle was God's object lesson to Israel and to the Church. Its main design was threefold. *First*, it was Jehovah's house set in the midst of His redeemed people. *Second*, it served as the scene and witness of various manifestations and revelations of God to man. *Third*, it also revealed the holy and righteous ground *(sacrifice)* and means—*(priesthood)*—by which men could in grace draw nigh to God. Now this latter consideration has been generally overlooked. Had it been borne in mind, the *seeming* disorder in the enumeration of the sacred vessels might easily be accounted for. Instead of *disorder* we have *perfection*. In those wondrous types and shadows, *why* is the Incense or Altar of Gold omitted in the description of the holy place? (xxv.) and *why* is the Laver not referred to in the account of the Court? (xxvii.). *Why* also are those two vessels fully described in chapter xxx., *after* the institution of the priesthood? (chaps. xxviii., xxix). The reasons are not far to seek. The worship of the people was conducted at the Golden Altar, and the practical cleansing of the priests—whether for worship inside or service outside—was an imperative necessity, and of this the Laver was the witness. Both were priestly vessels, and ere they could be brought into service, the priests had to be consecrated in order to use them. The priesthood, these vessels, and all that which specially pertained to them, were the divinely-appointed means by which a redeemed people could be brought to God in worship and service, hence the fitting place of these vessels after the institution of the priesthood. Practical purification and worship as God's priests are the respective thoughts conveyed by the Brazen Laver and Golden Altar. In the use of these, or rather what they symbolised, we draw nigh to God. We would call special attention to the fact that from chap. xxv. till chap. xxvii. 19 of Exodus we have as the grand and fundamental idea—God making Himself known to man; while in chaps. xxvii. 20 till xxx. it is the appointed means whereby men can approach God.

The Devotedness of the People.

The directions concerning the construction of the Taber-nacle, and the institution of priesthood—without which there could be no presentation to God of sacrifice at the Brazen Altar, or worship at the Golden Altar—are the subjects of seven chapters in Exod. xxv.-xxxi. How cheerfully and abundantly the "*willing* hearted"—both of men and women—contributed of their substance, and how truly the "*wise* hearted"—both men and women—wrought in the work till

all was completed, and Jehovah sanctified the Tabernacle
filling it with His glory, are the happy subjects of the last
six chapters of the book. The materials required for the
construction of the Tabernacle were collected by the
voluntary free-will offerings of the people. There was no
compulsion. All was a labour of love. The legal element,
giving or doing for reward, was conspicuous by its absence.
The motive spring was the enjoyed grace of Jehovah.
Exod. xxv. 1-9 ; xxxv. ; xxxvi. 1-7, form a piece of delightful reading—positively refreshing in these days of meanness
and mercenary motive.

All of Israel, from the youngest to the eldest, from the
poorest to the richest, but of Israel *only* are contemplated in
this bright scene of devotedness and service to Jehovah.
No stranger or alien from the commonwealth of Israel was
permitted to offer, or work in preparing a dwelling for
Jehovah. "And Moses spake unto all the congregation of
the children of Israel, saying, This is the thing which the
Lord commanded saying, Take ye *from among you* an
offering unto the Lord ; whosoever is of a willing heart, let
let him bring it, an offering of the Lord " (Exod. xxxv.4-5).
No one was asked to give. No solicitation, and no printed
list of donors. Jehovah's intervention on Israel's behalf
was the one and only worthy motive which led to the
devotedness of that day. Acts ii. is its counterpart in
Christian times. If Jehovah is to inhabit the praises of
Israel and dwell in the midst of His redeemed people, all
others are necessarily excluded. A saved people alone
can form God's habitation.

Where have *we* drifted to when the aid of the world is
invoked : its gold and silver eagerly sought, and the

patronage of the rich and great courted, but who, never-
theless, are the rejecters of our adorable Lord? "Know
ye not that the friendship of the world is enmity with
God?" (James iv. 4). In the present condition of things
the sharp and scriptural line of demarcation between the
Church and the world (2 Cor. vi. 14-18) is nigh obliterated.
The boundary wall of separation between the friends and
enemies of Jesus is in ruins. The Church as a whole has
deliberately abandoned the safe and holy ground of absolute
dependence on the Living God. She has ceased to lean on
an Almighty arm. The world has poured its gold into the
lap of a luxurious Church. The doors of the Sanctuary
are widely opened for the free admission of strangers to
God, who are invited, moreover to participate with
Christians in acts of "public worship." How contrary to
all this is the unworldly Christianity of early Apostolic
times. The company of the redeemed then, was both an
inclusive and exclusive one. It embraced the whole number
of believers: it was rigidly exclusive of men and things
not sanctified by the precious blood of Christ. What is
needed is not a reformed Church, but a distinct and positive
return to primitive Christianity.

In the construction of the Tabernacle there was work for
every member of the mighty host. Jehovah whom "the
Heaven of heavens cannot contain" desired to dwell
amongst men. He could have created for Himself a palace
outrivalling that of the Pharoahs' and one worthy of
His presence, but such His rich and condescending grace
that He would have the willing hearts and ready hands of
His redeemed people to prepare Him a home. "Let *them*
make Me a sanctuary that I may dwell among them." The

hearts of the people were deeply touched by the many signal displays of Jehovah's intervention on their behalf. Love was conspicuously displayed throughout the camp of Israel. It overflowed the banks and barriers of human selfishness. It had its spring in Jehovah Himself. Its strength and reality were proved by generous deeds. The grace of God was answered by the grace of the people, for right worthy was Jehovah to receive their love and wealth! Their hearts were freely opened, and their riches poured out morning after morning into the treasury. So fully and abundantly did the people respond to the alone claim of love that their generosity had to be restrained. "For the stuff they had was sufficient for all the work to make it, and *too much*" (xxxvi. 7).

"Too much!" In a somewhat lengthened period of about 55 years of happy service for our beloved Lord, we have only known of *one* instance in which on a certain occasion we had the unspeakable joy of crying "too much." We had to restrain the generous giving of many and assure the givers that the great need of those in whom we were interested had been abundantly met. Cheques were returned, for the need had been satisfied. Is the Lord's treasury now-a-days so filled to overflowing? Has the grace of God so reached our hearts that it has emptied our pockets? Is our wealth poured out at our Lord's feet? Is our love of such a self-sacrificing character, that we give not according to the giving of the rich, who cast into the treasury "of their abundance," but of the poor widow, who "of her penury hath cast in *all* the living that she had?" (Luke xxi.). Think you the poor widow whose only support was Jehovah would not be cared for by Him? Yea, verily!

If the worthiness of *Jehovah* wrought such wonders of grace amongst Israel of old, surely the worthiness of the *Lamb* ought to yield even a deeper form of devotedness in us! "Worthy is the Lamb to receive . . . riches."

If any were too poor to give, they could at least work. There was something for all—for every member of the mighty redeemed host of about two millions of people—something to *give* and to *do*.   It might not be much, but its acceptance by Jehovah was not according to the wealth of the giver, or the wisdom of the workman, but according to the *state* of the heart.   It is so now.   God loveth a cheerful giver.   The willing hearted gave.   The wise hearted wrought.   Intelligence, skill, and knowledge of Jehovah's requirements characterized these latter.   They wrought according to the pattern shown to Moses on the Mount and no deviation could be allowed, or amended plan be tolerated.   "God is jealous and the Lord revengeth" any affront on His glory or on His Word.   Jehovah Himself was the Architect of His own house, hence nothing was left to man's judgment, or to what he might consider best.   The whole was arranged and planned according to infinite wisdom.   The size, number, and other specifications of such small items, and mere matters of detail as pins, cords, hooks, and taches were divinely regulated.   What a lesson to us! Obedience to God must be rendered to Him not as we see fit, or in weighty matters only.   But obedience to Him is due at all times; do His will at all cost.   Our life as God's children in all its detail, ought to be a life of simple and prompt obedience.   We are not our own.   We are the blood-bought property of another.   We cannot make choice of a path of obedience.   We live only to do His will in all things

—great and small. We are sanctified to the obedience of Christ; to obey as He obeyed; to walk as He walked. A higher standard there could not be, and a lower one there must not be.

The Offerings of the People and Their Spiritual Signification.

" This is the offering which ye shall take of them:—

Gold
Silver } of *metals.*
Brass

Blue
Purple } of *colours.*
Scarlet

Fine Linen } of *fabrics.*
Goats' Hair

Rams' skins dyed red } of *coverings.*
Badgers' skins

Shittim Wood—*the only wood named.*

Oil } *for anointing and incense.*
Spices

Onyx Stones } *the Onyx alone named;*
Stones " } *many other stones—twelve at least.*

(Exod. xxv. 3-7).

The combined value of the foregoing offerings has been roughly estimated at £250,000—probably much more.

THEIR SPIRITUAL SIGNIFICATION.

Israel left Egypt a wealthy people. Its gold, silver, jewels, precious stones, rich and varied stores of raiment were poured in profusion into the lap of the departing people : while of course their numerous flocks and herds accompanied them into the wilderness (Exod. xi. 2, 3 ; xii. 32, 36).* Israel spoiled the Egyptians.

The materials so freely offered by the people are enumerated in Exodus, chap. xxv. 3-7, and are again named exactly in the same order in chap. xxxv. 5-9, when the work was about to commence.

In considering the typical import of these things we must avoid dogmatism. The spiritual signification of the materials employed in the construction of the Tabernacle must appeal to minds taught of God. We cannot enforce all these teachings with a "thus saith the Lord," but surely much and real instruction is gained by those whose spiritual instinct is wisely used (Heb. v. 14). The leading lines of truth are developed clearly enough in the Epistle to the Hebrews. Our spiritual understanding must fill in many of the details in this delightful branch of study ; but these details must be in moral keeping with the general line of truth as unfolded in the Epistle to the Hebrews.

Gold.—Christ in His Divine Nature. Essential Glory and Divine Righteousness. Christ the Eternal Son in the Divine glory and dignity of His Person.

---

*"Borrow" literally to *ask* or *demand*. Centuries of service demanded ample recompense which had been unrighteously withheld.

Silver.—Christ effecting Atonement and Redemption in the power and value of His own blood : see for Atonement, Exod. xxx. 12-16 ; for Redemption, Num. xviii. 16. It was the *Atonement* money that was used in the building of the Tabernacle—not the Redemption silver as is generally, but erroneously stated.

Brass, or native copper.—Christ bearing the judgment of sin—endurance and stability. His ability, because God, to bear the cross. *Gold* signifies Righteousness in the presence of God. *Brass*, Righteousness in judgment measured out according to human responsibility.

The colours were blue, purple, and scarlet which occur in this combination and order about 28 times in the book of Exodus.

Blue.—Christ the heavenly One on earth (1 Cor. xv. 47-48 ; John i. 18). The Nature of the Son as heavenly and Divine is inscrutable to all—only the Father knows Him (Matt. xi. 27).

Purple.—Christ in humiliation and death : see Num. iv. 13, for the meaning here given.

Scarlet.—Christ invested with the insignia of earth's glory : see Rev. xi. 15 ; Dan. vii. 14. Human glory.

The textile fabrics were fine linen and goats' hair.

Fine Linen.—Christ in spotless purity—practical righteousness, as exhibited by Christ in all His life and in all its detail, hence the challenge of the Righteous One " Which of you convinceth Me of sin "? (John viii. 46); see also Ps. xvii.

Goats' Hair.—Christ in prophetic character, and in practical separation from all evil without and within.

The coverings over all were rams' skins dyed red, and badgers' skins. Thus the order was as follows : first, set of fine linen curtains; second, set of goats' hair curtains; third, a covering of rams' skins dyed red ; fourth, over all a covering of badgers' skins. Two curtains and two coverings.

Rams' Skins Dyed Red.—Christ's devotedness to God even unto death. The ram was the consecration animal (Exod. xxix. 27). The skin of the *sin* offering was burned outside the camp (Lev. iv. 11, 12 ; Exod. xxix. 14). The skin ·of the *burnt* offering was given to the officiating priest (Lev. vii. 8). These rams' skins dyed red told of absolute surrender to God even to the death of the cross.

Badgers' Skins.—Christ in the absolute holiness of His Person and Life repelling every form of outward evil. To the natural eye and mind " no form nor comeliness."

The only wood referred to in the construction of the Tabernacle is the shittim. There are four kinds specified in the building of Solomon's Temple, namely, the cedar, fir, algum, and olive. In Ezekiel's Temple the palm tree, emblematic of *rest* and *victory*, is the only one named, and we may add, that neither gold, silver, nor brass are referred to in the millennial Temple of the prophet of the captivity.

Shittim Wood.—Christ in the incorruptibility of His human nature. In Him there was neither taint, nor corruption, nor sin. " That HOLY THING which shall be born of thee (the virgin) shall be called the Son of God " (Luke i. 35).

Oil, and spices, these latter were four in number (Exod. xxx. 34), answering to the four-fold description of Christ in the Gospels *i.e.*, the King, the Servant, the Man, the Son and Lamb of God.

Oil for the Light.—Christ the light of the world in the power of the Holy Ghost. The light is Christ; the oil is the Spirit.

Spices for Anointing Oil.—Christ in moral grace and beauty witnessed to by the Spirit.

Spices for Sweet Incense.—Christ in varied moral beauties and perfections displayed in His life here below, *now* filling heaven with fragrance.

The only stone specially named is the Onyx, but other precious stones were abundantly supplied though not here specified. "Onyx stones and stones to be set in the ephod and in the breastplate."

Onyx Stones.—Christ in many and varied excellencies.

Stones for the Ephod and Breastplate.—Christ in the many and diversified moral glories of His Person and ways manifested on behalf of His saints, and in which they appear before God.

Its Central Position in the Midst of Israel.

The Tabernacle when set up in the wilderness became the centre of the many thousands of Israel, and the meeting-place between Jehovah and His redeemed people (Exod. xxix. 42-46). *In* it God dwelt, and *out* of it He addressed His people in strains of richest grace (Lev. i. 1). It is several times termed "the Tabernacle of Witness," as eloquent in its testimony of heavenly and "better things to come."

The Tabernacle was erected, and set up in the wilderness on the first day of the first month of the second year of the deliverance from Egypt (Exod. xl. 2.)   Its flooring was the *sand* of the desert (Num. v. 17), unlike that of the Temple which was of pure *gold* (1 Kings vi. 30).   What mattered it whether sand or gold formed the floor of God's house.   It was *His* presence which made the sacred enclosure all glorious and holy ; which made it the most sacred and blessed spot on earth, for the glory of Jehovah *filled* it and the majesty of Jehovah abode *thereon* (xl. 34).

That sleeper wrapped in slumber in the apparently sinking vessel in the angry Galilean sea, is none other than the Rock of Ages and the Eternal God (Mark iv. 37-41). God in the midst is faith's answer to *all* the forces of evil— single or combined. His presence in the Tabernacle was the chief glory and strength of Israel. His presence in the Church is our Divine safeguard. Wreck and ruin, nations alarmed and armed, clouds and darkness, governments and powers may rock and reel, but all is still, all calm and peace within the charmed circle of the Lord's immediate presence.   Jehovah *in* the midst and Jehovah *on* the throne are enough till pilgrim days are over.

When the Tabernacle was finished the glory of Jehovah so filled the sacred enclosure that Moses the Mediator could not enter (Exod. xl. 35).   On the completion of the Temple the glory filled the house "so that the priests could not stand to minister" (1 Kings viii. 10, 11). When the new and spiritual house composed of *living* stones was formed, then the Spirit of God occupied it, with the result that every heart was stirred, and every tongue became eloquent in expressing the wonderful works of God (Acts ii.).

The Tabernacle with its Court set in the midst of the many thousands of saved and happy Israel, must have been an imposing sight—an all-absorbing object of interest to the whole nation, as also to each one of the mighty host. The tents of Moses, of Aaron and his sons, occupied the nearest position and were pitched on the front of the entrance—east (Num. iii. 38). Then the Levites surrounded the Court according to their respective families. "The Levites shall pitch round about the Tabernacle of testimony" Num. i. 53). The sons of Levi were Gershon, Kohath and Merari. This latter as a family was the more numerous of the three—probably because of the heavier work alloted to them. The boards, pillars, sockets of brass and silver which were the special care of the Merarites demanded constant relays of men, and these, because of their number were ever at hand. Gershon and his sons had their work and place assigned them on the west side of the Tabernacle. Kohath and his sons had also a weighty charge committed to them, and were pitched on the south side of the Tabernacle. Merari and his sons were by Divine appointment set to guard on the north side, while as we have already remarked, Moses, Aaron and his sons guarded the door of entrance on the east side of the Tabernacle (Num. iii.). The service of the Levites was not to be entered upon before thirty years of age nor to be extended beyond fifty years of age. Nor was the service in all to exceed twenty years (Num. iv.). These injunctions are six times repeated. The most vigorous period of life was thus absolutely devoted to God and to His service. Then the tribes of Israel were pitched " far off about the Tabernacle of the congregation " (Num. ii. 2)—three tribes on each side under their respective standards.

All was duly regulated and ordered by God. It was His house, and He alone had sovereign right to assign each one his place and prescribe the special work of each and all. God gives each one his place, assigns his work and regulates his service. Thus the whole nation and every individual thereof, were appointed guardians and custodians of the Tabernacle. Probably the people when at rest in their respective camps, formed a square of about twelve miles, and in the midst stood the Tabernacle to which all eyes and hearts were directed—the centre of their worship and out of which they were governed and directed. " Happy is that people that is in such a case; yea, happy is that people whose God is the LORD " (Ps. cxliv. 15).

God by His Spirit now dwells in the Church 1 Cor. iii. 16; Eph. ii. 22), and in each believer (1 Cor. vi. 19).

The Church is God's Temple—the Shrine of His holiness.

The Church is God's Habitation—for He dwells in it.

The Church is God's House—the sphere of His special government. The Temple, the Habitation, and the House are each composed of living stones, i.e., saved persons.

The Aaronic Priesthood.

Jehovah's sovereign choice of Israel as His people was founded on His absolute will and purpose. I AM THAT I AM. We can assign no reason for it. Israel was a Divine selection from amongst the nations and families of the earth (Amos iii. 2). But the people were sinful, absolutely ignorant of God, and in abject slavery and misery in Egypt. Jehovah rises to the occasion. He provides the blood of the Paschal Lamb as an answer to His own righteous judgment (Exod. xii.), crushes the strength of the enemy in the Red Sea (xiv.), and in the same act of Divine power redeems His people. The old bonds with sin and Satan were for ever broken, and the nation redeemed for the worship and service of Jehovah.

The calling of Israel to be a peculiar people to Jehovah Himself, was a privilege of the highest order and character, one founded solely on the sovereign choice of God, and hence irrevocable (Rom. xi. 29). On the Divine side all was safe. But on the human side this new and happy relationship, expressed in communion and intercourse with Jehovah had to be practically maintained. To effect this, priesthood as a standing institution in Israel was established—the normal link between the people and God.*

We may observe that the break down of the priesthood in the family of Eli as the means established by God to meet the failure and weakness of His people, only served as an occasion for our God to draw upon the resources in Himself. God, even our God, is ever more than equal to any difficulty. If that which was set up in Israel to meet failure, itself failed, what is the resource? God establishes prophecy in Samuel (Acts iii. 24), and by it He would address the conscience of the people and direct their thoughts onward to the glory of the Kingdom. But prophecy as an ordered institution of God miserably failed in the family of Samuel. There yet remained but one resource—one remedy —if the blessing of the people was to be secured and

---

*Worship is from *man* to God. Ministry is from *God* to man. In the exercise of the former we are regarded as priests ; whereas in the latter we act as servants. As priests we worship in the sanctuary ; as servants we minister in the church and in the world.

maintained; royalty was established in David. This means of blessing is one which stretches out to the world at large, not to Israel only. These three institutions, namely, Priesthood, Prophecy, and Royalty shall be witnessed in combined perfection in the palmy days of the Kingdom.* The connection between those three great principles of blessing are fully unfolded in the first book of Samuel.

ITS ESTABLISHMENT.

The institution of the priesthood is fully detailed in four chapters, Exod. xxviii., xxix. ; Lev. viii., ix. In the book of Exodus the subject of the priesthood is introduced between the numerous typical displays of *God* to man, and of those which signified *man's* approach to God. The revelation of priestly service and order, therefore, is just in its proper place, and affords another illustration of the perfection of the matchless volume of inspiration.

In the book of Leviticus the priesthood occupies an equally important place. In the first seven chapters, sacrifice is treated of in fulness of detail and wealth of spiritual significance. Sacrifice is the moral basis of priesthood. Had there been no sacrifice there could have been no priest. Not only did the one precede the other, but sacrifice formed the ground of all priestly service in the Court and Tabernacle. Intercession, worship, and com-

---

*The priest was set to meet all failure under the law. The prophet was to recall the obedience of the people to the law. The king was to uphold the authority of the law, and that by the exercise of royal power. While priesthood failed as the normal channel of blessing between the *nation* and God, it was yet available for *individual* faith.

munion were morally dependent upon and founded upon the Brazen Altar. Priestly discernment too was needed to maintain ceremonial purity in distinguishing the clean from the unclean, the holy from the unholy (chaps. x.-xv.), followed by a chapter which in its typical import is second to none in the Scriptures (xvi.). In chap. xvi. the fundamental truth of atonement in all its parts is regarded as the sole, special, and unique work of the high priest. The order therefore is first, sacrifice, then the priesthood based upon it, followed by priestly discernment so that no defilement hinder the freest intercourse with Jehovah, and lastly the making of atonement—a yearly work of immense value to Israel and of priceless worth to us viewed in its typical significance.

It may assist the reader in Tabernacle-study, to bear in mind that Aaron—Israel's first high priest—never prefigures Christians, but Christ our "Great High Priest." Aaron and his sons typify our happy association as priests and worshippers with Christ in the heavenly sanctuary. *All* Christians in this dispensation are constituted God's "*holy* priesthood" (1 Peter ii. 5), and God's "*royal* priesthood" (verse 9). As the former we offer up spiritual sacrifices to God; as the latter we display to others the virtues of God. Aaron and his house typify Christ and the whole priestly family—"whose house are we." The congregation of Israel signifies the nation then or future.

Levitical Service.

Priesthood was established in the family of Aaron, Levitical service in the tribe of Levi. Israel worshipped Jehovah through the intermediary service of the priest, and served Jehovah in the person and work of the Levite. In Leviticus the Tabernacle and the priest are prominent; whereas in Numbers the journeyings of the people and service of the Levites are the distinguishing truths. In both books, however, the Tabernacle is the centre of interest, whether for worship or service. Now, however, each Christian is both a priest and a Levite. He worships in the sanctuary and serves in the harvest-field. *All* believers are equally privileged to serve as priests and to serve as Levites. The two were separately regarded of old, in Christianity they are combined in each redeemed person.

"And the LORD spake unto Moses, saying, Bring the tribe of Levi near, and present them before Aaron the priest, that they may minister unto him. And they shall keep his charge, and the charge of the whole congregation before the tabernacle of the congregation, to do the service of the tabernacle. And they shall keep all the instruments of the tabernacle of the congregation, and the charge of the children of Israel, to do the service of the tabernacle. And thou shalt give the Levites unto Aaron and to his sons: they are wholly given unto him out of the children of Israel" (Num. iii. 5-9).

God has a just, a righteous claim upon His creatures on the double ground that He is the Creator and Preserver of all. He claimed all the first born of man and beast, both of Egypt and of Israel. The pride, the strength, the excellency of these nations, as expressed in the first born, were rightfully claimed by God; for judgment in the case of Egypt (Exod. xii. 29), for service in that of Israel (Num. iii. 12, 13). Jehovah took the Levites instead of the first born of redeemed

Israel. This tribe was to be wholly devoted to the service of Jehovah. Israel were redeemed for worship and service. This they did representatively through the priest and by the Levite. Has this not a voice to us? Are we not redeemed for a distinct and definite purpose? We *have* been saved at an infinite cost—saved to worship in the sanctuary above, and to serve in the harvest-field below.

Levitical service was exercised within an exceedingly narrow sphere. In chapter iv. of the book of Numbers we learn that the service was confined to the Tabernacle. Judaism was essentially a conservative system. It was so even in the time of our Lord (Matt. x. 5, 6). Christianity on the contrary knows no limitations. The whole world is its sphere of operation, and every creature the subject of its glorious ministry.

In the passage which we have transcribed from the third chapter of Numbers, we have unfolded a deeply interesting feature of Levitical service. " Bring the tribe of Levi near and present them before Aaron the priest, that they may *minister unto him.*"

The Levites were given to Aaron and his sons (verse 9), thus maintaining an inseparable connection between worship and service. Our work on earth should correspond to our place on high. But besides this general truth, the Levites were to " minister unto him." Aaron represents our great High Priest in the heavenly sanctuary. We serve *Him.* He represents us in heaven. We serve Him on earth. Our place in heaven must not be divorced from our walk on earth. All we do here should have a heavenly character stamped upon it. Just as the Levites served Aaron so we serve Christ. We as associated with Him in heaven in worship, serve Him down here. We morally connect heaven and earth. We bring the savour and communion of heaven to our walk and service on earth. We in our service down here minister to Him up there. The High Priest ministers for us in the presence of God, and we here minister to Him. This consideration gives an elevated character to our service.

Our conflict is in heavenly places (Eph. vi. 12), our citizenship is in heaven (Phil. iii. 20). Levitical service was connected with the Tabernacle, yet outside the sanctuary but in moral connection with it. So in like manner our service while performed down here, has or should have a heavenly character imprinted upon it. We serve Him Who is in the heavenly sanctuary and do it with the savour of the place where He is, impressed upon all we do—may God grant it!

The Court.

In the detailed description of the Tabernacle and its vessels and services, the sacred historian commences from *within*, describing separately the Ark and the Mercy-seat (Exod. xxv. 10-22) in the holiest or innermost part of the sacred building. Then the vessels in the holy place are detailed, with the exception of the Golden or Incense Altar (verses 23-40); next, the Tabernacle itself, with its curtains, coverings and boards; the dividing veil and door being minutely described (chap. xxvi.). Then the Court with its pillars, sockets, hangings, and gate are delineated with an exactness equal to any part of the holy edifice. But, again, we have an omission of an important vessel which stood in the Court; we refer to the Brazen Laver. Now the two omitted vessels, namely the Golden Altar and the Brazen Laver, were pre-eminently priestly vessels—none but priests could use them—hence the description of them (xxx.) comes *after* the institution of the priesthood (xxviii., xxix.), and rightly so. In this connection we may remark that the two vessels which stood in the Court were both of brass : the Brazen Altar and the Brazen Laver. Only in the former the brass covered the shittim wood ; whereas the latter was wholly of brass. There is too a very intimate connection between the two vessels. Both were for the judgment of sin. At the Altar the sinner had his sins judged according to his responsibility as such. At the Laver the worshipper had his uncleanness judged according to his responsibility as such. In fact, the Court with all in it, had as its distinguishing feature, *Righteousness.* The hangings, vessels, sockets, all told the same tale and proclaimed the same truth, that righteousness must be maintained and upheld whether for saint or sinner. The vessels then in the Court would express the ground, place, and means by which God could righteously meet any sinner coming out of the world and meet him too in grace,

As to the general construction of the Tabernacle we shall begin from the *outside*, first looking at the Court (xxvii. 9-18). The Court was not covered. The heavens formed its covering. Angels from above were no doubt interested spectators of what took place—" which things the angels desire to look into." The Court with its flooring of sand or dust was 100 cubits, or 150 feet in length ; and 50 cubits, or 75 feet in breadth, that is 18 inches to the sacred cubit. There is considerable diversity of opinion as to the English measurement of the cubit, but it is not a matter of importance. There is no moral teaching involved whether you make 18 or 22 inches to the cubit. The civil cubit was about 22 inches.

One hundred cubits (150 feet) of fine twined linen were suspended on 20 pillars for the north side of the Court, and the same for the south side. These pillars were of shittim-wood, although not expressly stated. The shittah tree is named 26 times in the Scriptures, and only in the books of Moses. This wood was an exceedingly durable one, and grew plentifully in the great Arabian desert. Whether these pillars were formed square or round we are not told. The only other materials of a hard nature were brass. gold and silver. The pillars were not of brass, as Exod. xxxviii. 29-31 shew, nor were they of silver, for that metal was only used in the upper and ornamental parts, whilst gold was employed in covering the boards of the Tabernacle, and in the construction of certain vessels inside, but not in the Court. These pillars, therefore were of necessity shittim wood, resting on sockets of brass. The linen hangings were suspended by hooks of silver, while the fillets, or connecting rods, were also of silver. Between each of the pillars there were five cubits of linen hangings.

On the west side there were ten pillars, each supporting five cubits of hangings. On the east side, in the centre, stood the gate of the Court, termed a "door" in Num. iii. 26, formed of 20 cubits of fine twined linen suspended on four shittim-wood pillars; while on either side of the gate were three pillars, supporting 15 cubits of linen—five for each pillar.

Thus on the north side (the right hand) were 20 pillars; on the south side (the left hand) 20 pillars; on the west side

10 pillars; and on the east 10 pillars—in all 60 pillars of shittim-wood.

The shittim-wood has been termed "the imperishable or incorruptible wood," and sets forth the incorruptible human nature of our Lord (Luke i. 35). The pillars, His stability and firmness as man. The linen, His righteous character. The sockets of brass were unseen, signifying His ability to sustain Divine judgment. The silver, the grace of God in providing atonement by Christ's most precious blood. The blue tells of His heavenly character, the purple reminds us of His sufferings and death, whilst the scarlet proclaims His coming glory in connection with the earth. Christ is both the gate and door of the Court. On the four sides of the Court the righteous character of Christ towards the world was expressed, and of this the four Gospels are the witness.

The height of the curtained enclosure, five cubits (7½ feet), effectually precluded an outsider from witnessing what went on in the court, which was *a* holy place (Lev. vi. 16, 26, not "*the* holy place," as in Authorised Version). Besides, the Levites—the jealous custodians of the sacred vessels and ministers of the sanctuary—were set to keep, watch, and guard all round the Court. A man must be born again ere he can see "the kingdom of God" (John iii. 3), and ere he can enter it (verse 5). So the inside of the Court and of the Tabernacle, could neither be seen nor entered from outside; all being effectually screened from the public gaze and protected from unhallowed approach. There was no entrance save by the door on the east. You might wander round about the building, but not too near, for all was holy, and the ever watchful and jealous guardians—the Levites—were ever on duty. Now, however, we enter the sacred enclosure.

When *outside*, those white curtains telling of purity were our fear and dread. But now *inside*, those same curtains are our safeguard and security. It makes all the difference whether we are outside or inside. Outside, Divine righteousness is a terror to a guilty sinner. Inside, Divine righteousness is the sinner's boast. Inside, you look around on those curtains which speak to you of Christ. The pillars which support them are firm and immoveable. Their sockets were of brass ; their fillets of silver. Christ bearing Divine judgment is the basis *(brass)*. The blood of atonement (Lev. xvii. 11 ; Exod. xxx. 11-16) secures all above *(silver)*. The chapiters, or ornamental upper parts of the pillars, were overlaid with silver. There is beauty as well as security. The curtains were attached to the pillars by hooks of silver, shewing that righteousness for us, or on our behalf, is inseparable from the blood of atonement—the precious blood of Christ. The filleting of the pillars above with silver kept them firm and steady. Thus secured at the base by brazen sockets, and bound together above by silver fillets, the pillars in turn sustained the curtains. Storms might sweep through the desert, but the Court stood firm and steady as a rock. God established it. Are you in the Court as a *true* believer, or as a *mere* professor ?

The Gate of the Court.

There could be no entrance to the Court and its privileges, save by the gate on the east side of the curtained enclosure. God's way to His own house was by that gate and that only. The Ritualist, the Rationalist, the mere Religionist is each seeking to deny the very essence, the kernal of Christianity, that Christ *alone* is the door of salvation (John x. 9). "Neither is there salvation in any other: for there is none other name under heaven given among men wherey we must be saved" (Acts iv. 12). Re-examine the foundations of your faith, dear reader, and see to it that Christ and not ordinances, Christ and not nature, Christ and not baptism, Christ and not experience, Christ and not works is your soul's only confidence in light of eternal judgment and wrath to come. The gate admitted to *outward* privileges in the Court.

The hangings for the gate of the Court were of the same material as the door of the Tabernacle, and the veil of the holiest, namely, fine twined linen; the colours, too, blue (His *heavenly character*), purple (His *sufferings*), and scarlet (His *glory*), were the same in the gate, door, and veil. The colours were wrought into the texture of the linen. Cherubim, emblematic of the moral attributes of God's throne centred in and exercised by Jesus (Ps. lxxxix. 14; John v. 22, 27), were wrought in the veil, and in the curtained roof of the Tabernacle, in keeping with the character of truth signified in these typical teachings. The cherubic figures were wanting in the hangings of the Court, and in the door of the Tabernacle. These types, and lights, and shadows afford us numerous glints and gleams of Christ in His Person, atoning sacrifice, and priestly and regal glories.

The hangings were suspended on four pillars, probably of shittim-wood; their sockets were of brass, the hooks and fillets above being of silver, reminding us again of the need of the blood of *Atonement* (Exod. xxx. 11-16). What met the eye outside was one unbroken line of white linen

—Christ, the Righteous and Holy One. But the eye is relieved, and the soul rests in the thought as the wide gate of the Court comes into view: Can I get within that righteous enclosure? Yes, for why the gate? Why the door? for both terms are employed to express the entrance to the Court. The gate expresses *judgment*, there it was administered, and is so still in the east (Exod. xxxii. 27; Gen. xix. 1). The door was for *admission* simply. Typically, Christ is both the gate and the door. In Him sin is judged, hence external privilege, as hearing the Word, the presence of the Spirit, etc.; by Him alone we enter the Court.

The gate stood on the east side of the Court, exactly in the centre. As the breadth of the Court was 50 cubits, or 75 feet, and the gate was 30 feet in width, it left $22\frac{1}{2}$ feet on either side of the gate. The gate of the Court was broad, the door of the Tabernacle was narrow, so also that of the veil dividing the holy, from the most holy. *Many* is the thought in the former; *few* is suggested by the two latter. The people thronged the Court, the priests alone could enter through the door into the holy place, while Aaron the high priest and Moses the Mediator, could alone enter the holiest.

But whilst the gate of the Court was wider than that of the door and veil, the same quantity of fine twined linen, 100 cubits or 150 feet, were required to make the gate, to make the door, and to make the veil. The same quantity for each. But these latter *i.e.*, the door and veil, were twice the height of the gate, being each 15 feet, so that the exact quantity of fine linen was the same in the three. The gate, the door, and the veil each told the story of Christ.

He is the gate into the Court of holy privilege. *He* is the door—the new and living way for the worshippers into the heavenly places. *He* is the veil into the immediate presence of God. The three doors exactly faced each other, and each spoke of Him Who said "I am the Door."

> "*Finish'd* all the types and shadows of the ceremonial law,
> *Finish'd* all that God had promised : death and hell no more shall awe.
>> *It is finish'd,*
> Saints from hence your comfort draw."

The Brazen Altar.

Having entered the Court by its one and only door, we now approach the Brazen Altar, fully described in the first eight verses of chap. xxvii.; emphatically "*the* Altar," called "the table of the Lord" (Mal. i. 12). What was laid thereon was fed upon by Jehovah, and is termed "the bread of their God." There were Altars from earliest times, the first mentioned being that built by Noah. But neither shape nor size of those Altars are specified. Altars might be made of earth or stone. If the latter, the stones were to be rough and unhewn; no human tool employed in shaping or beautifying, and, further, no steps were to be made. The Altars were to be level with the ground (Exod. xx. 24-26). The Altar of Judaism typifies the Cross of Christianity. The Cross of shame is our glory. It needs no human art to add to its beauty. The Cross in itself, and by itself stands alone.

> "In the Cross of Christ I glory,
>> Tow'ring o'er the wrecks of time ;
> All the light of sacred story
>> Gathers round its head sublime."

The heathen embellished their Altars with gold and precious stones.*

The Altar of *earth* would be a contemptible sight, in contrast to the Altar of the heathen adorned and beautified, but the worshippers as they gathered round the Altar of earth or one of unhewn and rough stone, could count upon the presence and blessing of Jehovah. " In all places where I record My Name *I will come unto thee and I will bless thee.*" Not the Altar of gold *inside*, but the Altar of brass *outside*, was the basis of the Levitical system. What the Cross is to Christianity, that the Brazen Altar was to Judaism. All sacrifice was offered on this Altar, the sacrificial animals being killed by the offerer on the north side (Lev. i. 11). On it the various prescribed parts of the victims were laid, and consumed by fire as a sweet savour to Jehovah.

In the case of the burnt offering (Lev. i.), and peace or communion offering (iii.), the officiating priest *sprinkled* the blood round about upon the Altar, but in that of the sin offerings (iv.), a deeper, more intense, and fuller action of the blood was called for. In these latter the blood was sprinkled before the veil, then put on the four horns of the Golden, or Incense Altar, or on those of the

---

* A SILVER ALTAR *(July 23, '08).*—" The Queen yesterday visited the premises of Messrs Barkentin and Krall, goldsmiths, of Regent Street, to inspect the great silver altar made for the Lady Chapel of St. Mark's, Philadelphia. The Altar, which is 7ft. long, 2ft. deep, and 3ft. 3ins. high, was designed and carried out at their works which are close to their showrooms. It was in hand for nearly four years." The *thing* is of silver. What about that which it is supposed to represent? Christ and Him crucified is our glory and boast. Our object is Christ, not an Altar of silver, nor the Cross as ornament.

Brazen Altar, according to the nature of the case, and the rest of the blood *poured* out at the bottom of the Altar. Then two lambs were to be offered daily on the Altar—one in the morning, 9 o'clock, the other in the evening, 3 o'clock (Exod. xxix. 38-42). These burnt offerings were to be accompanied by a flour offering, with *equal proportions* of oil and wine. Thus God would have daily prefigured before Him the life and death of His Son, while our joy (*wine*) consequent thereon, is ever in exact ratio to the Spirit's action (*oil*).

The Altar was four-square : a world-wide aspect and application surely, as the Cross undoubtedly is, and as the numeral four signifies. It was five cubits, or $7\frac{1}{2}$ feet in length and the same in breadth. Its height was three cubits, or $4\frac{1}{2}$ feet, the Mercy-seat just half that. The size of the Ark in length and height was exactly half the size of the Altar in these two respects. It was made of shittim-wood, the only wood used in the construction of the Tabernacle, and covered over with brass or native copper. It was made hollow, and exactly half-way down there was inserted a network of brass, on which were placed the sacrifices. Its four horns were also of brass, to which the animals were bound by cords (Ps. cxviii. 27). The blood upon the horns of the Altar spoke of absolute security. The moral strength and power of the Altar constitute a grand refuge and protection to those who cling to it. A *horn* implies strength. The four blood-sprinkled horns tell of Divine security from the righteous judgment of God.

The Cross, like the Altar, may be distinguished into two parts—Christ as the martyr suffering for righteousness (Ps. lxix.), and Christ as the victim agonizing for sin

(Ps. xxii.). The crucifixion of the Lord was commenced at the third hour (9 a.m., English time), and finished about the ninth hour (3 p.m., English time), thus fulfilling the type of the morning and evening sacrifice. Those six hours, like the Altar with its two parts, may be distinguished. The first three hours were mainly characterized by man's infliction of suffering; the second three hours of darkness, were specially marked by the endurance of Divine wrath on account of sin.

> " O love of God, O sin of man,
>   In this dread act your strength is tried,
>   And victory remains with love ;
>   For He our Love, is Crucified."

The five cubits of righteousness held up to view between the pillars round the Court, prove in type what is doctrinally stated in Rom. iii., "There is none righteous; no not one," but our failed responsibility to be righteous, is answered in the five cubits of judgment, borne by another for us. Righteousness in *life* expressed in the five cubits of linen. Righteousness in *judgment* shewn in the five cubits in the Altar. Judgment borne according to human responsibility. The Brazen Altar is God dealing in righteousness—judicial righteousness.

The Altar was made of shittim-wood, termed in the Septuagint or lxx., "incorruptible wood," thus pointing to the incorruptible humanity of our Lord, but the wood was overlaid with brass, the only metal which could stand fire ; so in this we witness the Divine ability of Christ to endure the fierce and unrelenting fire of judgment. Here then we have the infinite basis on which all sacrifice rests. That "Holy Thing" which was born of the virgin was incorruptible. As absolutely perfect in the womb of the virgin, as in the bosom of the Father, He had thus in Himself an infinite capacity to endure the expressed judgment of God. Christ was both Altar and Sacrifice.

The network of brass inserted half-way down in the hollow of the Altar—inside—one-and-a-half cubits down, reminds us of the internal sorrows of the Lord which are unspeakable. "His *soul* was made an offering for sin." The network was attached to four brass rings. On this net the sacrificial victims were laid and bound to the four projecting horns of the altar. "Bind the sacrifice with cords even to the horns of the altar." The appointed victim was held for death. Blood, the witness of death, was put on the horns of the Brazen Altar (Lev. iv. 25), for the sin of a ruler or one of the common people, also on those of the Golden Altar in the case of a priest or the congregation sinning (verses 7, 18). Thus blood meets the *offerer* in the Court, and the *worshipper* in the Tabernacle.

The sin of Judah was "graven on the horns of their Altars"* (Jer. xvii. 1). Either our sin or His blood which blots it out, is on God's Altar: which is it? The breadth of the Mercy-seat corresponded exactly to the height of the part of the Altar whereon the victim was laid. The blood was shed at the Altar, some of it being also sprinkled on the Mercy-seat. God's appreciation of the sacrifice is the measure of reception at the Mercy-seat. The sacrifice of Christ is towards the human race, hence the size of the Altar as exceeding other Tabernacle vessels—Ark, Table, etc. The pans, shovels, basins, flesh-hooks, and fire-pans were all made of the same

---

*The Brazen Altar in the Court, and the Altar of Gold in the Tabernacle.

fire-enduring metal ; they were accessories to the Altar of judgment, and intimate in their uses and offices, how awful, inconceivably awful was the agony endured by God's appointed Lamb.* How thorough ! how unsparing the judgment endured by Christ, else these vessels would not have been employed.

The staves of the Altar—of shittim-wood and brass—would signify the journeying character of the Altar. Carry it far and near, from pole to pole. Tell it out, tell it out to the nations, that Christ is God's sacrifice for a ruined world.

> " Sound His praises, tell the story—
>   Of Him who was slain.
> Sound His praises, tell with gladness—
>   He cometh again."

The Altar in Solomon's Temple—built wholly of brass—was much larger than the Tabernacle Altar, being thirty feet in length and breadth, and fifteen feet in height (2 Chron. iv. 1). The Altar was approached by an ascent as steps were forbidden (Exod. xx. 26). Solomon's Altar had no staves : they were not needed, its journeys being over. Rest was enjoyed and glory too.

> " We rear no Altar—Thou hast died :
>   We deck no priestly shrine ;
> What need have we of creature aid ?
>   The power to save is Thine."

The vital connection between the presence of God (the Tabernacle) and sacrifice, the ground of approach (the Altar), is indicated in the position of the Brazen Altar.

Pans for the ashes. *Shovels* to remove the ashes. *Basins* to receive the blood. *Flesh-hooks* to turn or remove the sacrifices. All these were made of brass—the great fire-enduring metal.

"Thou shalt set the Altar of the burnt offering *before* the door of the tabernacle of the tent of the congregation" (Exod. xl. 6). The effort of Satan in the down-grade movement, is to remove the Altar (the *Cross*) from its rightful place in the Court as the ground of approach to God, to deny that great and vital truth of God's Word taught to Israel in type and to us in repeated statements, that God cannot be approached, heaven cannot be entered, save on the ground of atonement, but which in His love and righteousness He has provided. To deny this, is really to tread in the way of Cain, who was the first to attempt the impossible, namely, to reach God by brushing aside the atonement. We reiterate the statement, emphasise the declaration that "WITHOUT SHEDDING OF BLOOD IS NO REMISSION." Sacrifice, even the sacrifice of Christ on the Cross, is a necessity of Divine righteousness, if God is to be glorified and sinners saved. The basis—grand and solid— on which alone God can meet and save a guilty sinner is THE CROSS. It is, thank God, an imperishable ground of safety, but it is the only one.

Standing beside the Altar, the individual Israelite would learn the blessed truth that, sinner as he was, God could righteously accept him, because of the value of the sacrifice which was wholly consumed on the Altar (Lev. i.)— not accepted *in* it, for "it shall be accepted for him" (verse 4). There is no such thought in Scripture as "I died *in* my substitute," or "I died *in* Him." Such language sets aside the true idea of substitution, which is not one *in* another, but one *for* another.

"The fire shall ever be burning upon the Altar; it shall never go out" (Lev. vi. 13), tells us that the remembrance

of Calvary is eternal.   The place called Calvary, where love
strove in agony and achieved its mightiest victory, is too
grand to perish from memory.   The thrilling story of the
Cross shall continue to bow the heart and knee of millions in
glory.   Then the sin-sacrifices, (unlike those contained in
chaps. i.-iii. of Leviticus) compulsory, were also laid on
the Altar of burnt-offering.   "And the priest shall make
an atonement for his sin that he hath committed, and it
shall be forgiven him " (chap. iv.).   In the burnt offering,
which presents the highest character of sacrifice, God's
glory in respect to sin was fully secured.   Christ in death
accomplishing the will and glory of God where sin
abounded and seemed to triumph, is the New Testament
truth of the burnt-offering.   By it the *acceptance* of the
person was secured.   By the sin-offering *forgiveness* of
sins was guaranteed.

But a further blessing was enjoyed by those congregated
beside, or at the Brazen Altar.   Jehovah at the door of the
Tabernacle met with and spoke to His people (Exod. xxix.
42), fitting place for them to hear the words of Jehovah.
In the consideration of the Altar three distinguishing
truths appear: The Lord Himself is our Altar ; Christ
Himself our Sacrifice ; Christ Himself our Great High
Priest.

The Brazen Laver.

We next approach the Laver, of which neither size nor
shape are given (xxx. 18-21).   This is the last vessel named,
the first mentioned is the Ark.   The Laver was made

wholly of brass. There was no brass *in* the Tabernacle. Gold *inside*, brass *outside*. Divine righteousness *in* the sanctuary ; Divine righteousness according to human responsibility *outside* the sanctuary. The Laver does not seem to have been covered in preparation for the journeys of the wilderness; all the other vessels were. Its omission in this connection is significant (Num. iv. 1-14). Christ in His life down here in ABSOLUTE HOLINESS is a fact. *Covered ?* Never. He ever lived in the sight of God, of angels, of men. His life in all its wondrous detail lay open to all. It was never a covered life, whether at rest or journeying. His Person inscrutable, His life open and transparent to all.

In the Temple there were ten Lavers of brass, each resting on its own base. Each Laver was six feet in length and breadth and four-and-a-half feet in height. Five of the Lavers were placed north and five south. Then there was constructed a "molten sea" of huge size (1 Kings vii. 23-39).

The use and place of the Laver in the Court are highly significant. It was made of the polished brazen-mirrors of the women of Israel ; they, as well as the men, had right and privilege to assemble in the Court and enjoy and profit by the privileges which it afforded (Exod. xxxviii. 8). The Laver was filled with water, in which the priests washed hands and feet before ministering *at* the Altar or *in* the Tabernacle. It was a fitting act, therefore, in those women to part with those natural looking-glasses where beauty and self were rated at each one's own value, for God's one and only true looking-glass for one and all—the Word of God (James i.

23-25). The Laver was for the practical purification of
God's priests. It was the means of purification for
communion with God and of service for Him. Hands and
feet—acts and ways—must be kept clean for sanctuary
service. "Be ye clean that bear the vessels of the Lord,"
and so imperative was the command for ceremonial purity
on the part of God's priests and ministers of old, that the
penalty of death was annexed to any neglect of it (chap.
xxx. 17-21).

The Laver was filled with water, not with blood.
Blood on the Altar—*water* in the Laver. The daily
cleansing of our walk and ways is by the practical application of the Word to the soiled conscience. There was blood
on and at the Altar. It was water which filled the Laver.
The Altar was for the sinner. The Laver for the priests, and
this latter, *all* believers are in this dispensation (Heb. x. 22;
1 Pet. ii. 5, 9). Now the Altar was first approached, and
Divine teaching (typical) learnt there as to the meaning,
value, and application of the blood. There the sinner was
forgiven, and there he was accepted on the ground of the
atoning sacrifice. But as a priest and for sanctuary-service,
the Laver was indispensable. The priests were washed all
over once, an act never repeated, but the practical cleansing
by the water in the Laver was daily, constantly needful.

Christ as revealed in the Word, is the measure of our
practical cleansing. Christ in Whom too, the Word is embodied is the standard of daily walk for a believer. But
who can estimate at its value that infinite purity—inward
and outward—in nature and life—of Him Who was the
Brazen Laver, with its foot on a sin stained earth, yet
remained alone in absolute holiness?

"His life was pure, without a spot,
And all His nature clean."

Hence the Laver has no measurements, we are simply informed of the place it occupied—between the Altar and the Tabernacle ; the material of which it was made— brass ; and the use to which it was appointed— the purification of the priests. The Lord no doubt alluded to the Laver in His significant action recorded in John xiii. as He does, without doubt, to the Temple in chapter xiv.

The Brazen Altar and Brazen Laver both speak of the searching character of Divine judgment, whether it be of the sins of the sinner (the Altar), or the failure of the believer (the Laver). The Altar is sin judged by the Cross. The Laver is sin judged by the Word of God. Practical holiness, the maintenance of a good conscience by saint and minister, is absolutely essential for the enjoyment of communion with God, for worship in the heavenlies, and for service in the Church and in the world. The Laver is Christ viewed as a Divine person here below. It was made wholly of Brass—no shittim-wood. The water is the Word directing us to Him. The Laver was not measured, so Christ is the absolute measureless standard of holiness for His priests, His people. The Altar (the *Cross*) having done its work in perfecting the conscience for ever (Heb. x. 14) there can be no return to it save as a worshipper. To the Laver there is. The practical purification of our walk and conduct, was never more needful than now, when a correct creed or no creed is insisted upon, and loose walk and ways regarded as of little account.

General Structure of the Tabernacle.

This had better be understood ere with uncovered head and unshod feet we enter it. A full and accurate description is furnished us in chaps. xxvi. and xxxvi. of Exodus. It stood on the west side of the Court in a line with the gate. The solid framework was composed of forty-eight boards, twenty north, twenty south, six west, with a corner board at each end. These boards were of shittim-wood overlaid with gold—the human and Divine natures of our Lord. Each individual board expressed the same vital and fundamental truth. We see Christ in the structure as a whole, and Christ in each of the boards. *Not* believers, but Christ and Christ only. The boards were ten cubits (15 feet) in length, and one cubit and a half in breadth. Thus the breadth of each board was the exact height of the Mercy-seat (chap. xxxvii. 6), and also of each of the two parts of the Brazen Altar, divided by the brazen network on which the sacrificial victim was laid (chap. xxvii. 1, 5). Christ in the combined glory of His Person—Divine and Human—is the truth represented in each board. The infinite capacity of Christ to bear Divine judgment, is taught us in the Brazen Altar. The Mercy-seat of gold sprinkled with the blood of atonement, is Christ on high in righteousness and glory, before Whom, and in Whose holy presence, we are privileged to stand without fear.

> " *Hither*, then, your music bring,
>   Strike aloud each tuneful string ;
>   Mortals join the hosts above,
>   Join to praise redeeming love."

The north and south sides of the Tabernacle were each composed of twenty boards. Thus the length of the holy building would be thirty cubits (45 feet), the boards being a cubit and a-half in breadth. Its height was ten cubits (15 feet). Its width was exactly the same, namely, ten cubits (15 feet). Each board was maintained in its place by two tenons, or hands, which again were grasped by two sockets of silver. Two sockets under each of the 48 gold-covered boards are 96, then there was a socket under each of the four pillars supporting the beautiful veil—in all 100 sockets of silver (xxvi. 15, 25, 32). The quantity of silver used for the sockets and ornamental parts of the pillars is stated in chap. xxxviii. 25-28. Sustaining the Court there were 60 pillars, each resting on a base or socket of brass, hooks and fillets above being of silver. The door of the tent was suspended on five pillars each resting on a socket of brass—this gave 65 sockets of brass. Then in order to bind the boards in one compact body of strength and security, five bars of shittim-wood covered with gold—same as the boards—ran along the two sides, and also along the end at the west; fifteen bars in all being inserted in rings of gold attached to the boards. The third or middle bar stretched across the whole length of the building—45 feet; of the length of the other cross-bars we are not informed.

The middle bar unlike the others was made "to shoot *through* the boards from the one end to the other" (xxxvi. 33). This peculiar arrangement must have added greatly to the strength and security of the building. Thus inside and outside, through and through it was one inseparable compact whole. The unity in the Person of the Lord—the unity of nature and attribute—is our strength as we contemplate our blessing in the duality of His Person and Wondrous Being. What wonders and mysteries are wrapped up in Him Whose "Name shall be called Wonderful, Counsellor, the Mighty God, the Everlasting Father, the Prince of Peace" (Isa. ix. 6). The corner boards at the extreme end—north and south—were coupled together at top and bottom by rings of gold, in addition to the tenons and silver sockets at the base. These corner boards then would knit the ends so firmly by their fastening of rings, tenons, and sockets, or blocks of silver, that a break-down was impossible, while the sides were equally upheld and maintained by the bars.

The boards may have been coupled—board to board —at the top as the corner boards were, but of this we are not informed. The cross bars would be sufficient no doubt. Here then we have the Rock of Ages embodied in the Tabernacle. The Person of the Lord in Divine and Human nature—the gold and wood—is the mighty basis of our faith. Divine right to the throne of the Eternal was His, yet He stooped as man to the death of the Cross. The Lord Jesus Christ in the double glory of His person— in His two-fold nature—Deity and Humanity—is the grand basis of Christianity. It is on Him the Cross rests. What a tower of strength and rock of salvation we have in the contemplation of our Divine and adorable Lord and Saviour.

> "JOIN all the glorious names
>   Of wisdom, love, and power,
>   That mortals ever knew,
>   That angels ever bore :
> All are too mean to speak His worth.
> Too mean to set my Saviour forth."

Then over this fast, firm, and solid frame-work four coverings were spread, each setting forth Christ in a distinct and special character.

The Door of the Tabernacle.

We must now direct attention to the door of God's dwelling place. It stretched across the whole of the east side. The door was formed of the same material as the hangings of the Court, of the gate, of the veil, and of the Tabernacle curtains, namely, fine linen, emblematic of the personal purity of Christ—His righteous character before men (the Court), and in presence of God (the veil). The colours, blue, purple, and scarlet, were *not* wrought in the hangings of the Court, but were in the gate, door, veil, and beautiful curtains. Cherubic figures were skilfully wrought into the texture of the linen (in addition to the colours) in the veil, and in the Tabernacle curtains, but omitted in the gate, and door, and hangings of the Court. The moral supports of God's throne as justice and judgment (Ps. lxxxix. 14)—judicial authority—are seen in that which specially presents Christ in the presence of God. The Cherubim whether on the Ark, in the curtains, or in the veil could only be seen inside.

The five pillars of shittim-wood overlaid with gold (the union of the Divine and Human natures in the Person of our Lord), were to support the display of needle work wrought in the pure linen. What a tale *that* door unfolds! We are satisfied that the shittim-wood in the Altar, in the pillars here, in the staves, and in the Ark can only set forth the perfect human nature of our Lord—holy and incorruptible. It is not a gain but loss to force the shittim-wood to utter any name but that of Christ. In the *five* pillars there may be an allusion to the five Christ-given ministries of

Eph. iv. 11. Surely the only business of apostle, prophet, evangelist, pastor, and teacher is in their several spheres to point to the curtained door, containing in hieroglyphic characters the history of Christ as righteous, as heavenly, in death, and on the throne, all wrapped up in the mystery of His Being as *One*.

The beautiful hangings were of needlework. The variegated glories of Christ were, so to speak, wrought into the very texture of that marvellous holy life. These glories are inseparably attached to His Person, as the hangings to the pillars by hooks of gold. Divine righteousness linked and secured all together. Gold, too, adorned the chapiters, or ornamental upper parts of the pillars. Five brass sockets at the base maintained the pillars immovable in their position. As you are about to enter the Tabernacle solemnly remember that you can only do so on the ground that Divine righteousness has judged sin in "the place called Calvary." The gold at the top of the pillars signifies Divine righteousness in itself; while the brass at the base of the pillars shews the inflexibility of Divine righteousness judging sin. The Court-pillars had silver above and brass beneath; here we have gold above and brass beneath.

The Beautiful White Linen Curtains.

(Exod. xxvi. 1-6; xxxvi. 8-13).

These curtains were ten in number, each curtain being twenty-eight cubits long and four cubits broad. Pure white linen formed the ground-work on which the colours blue, purple, and scarlet were displayed, as also the highly significant hieroglyphic figures of the Cherubim. The colours were wrought by the wise-hearted women into the very texture of the linen and wrought by hand. The Cherubim were of special work and design (xxvi. 1). Both men and women had their part in the preparation of the materials which formed the roof of God's dwelling place.

Those pure linen curtains are termed " one Tabernacle " (verse 6). The goats' hair curtains are spoken of as one Tent (verse 11). The rams' skins dyed red, and badgers' skins are termed " coverings " (verse 14). Thus the curtains and coverings are respectively termed, Tabernacle, Tent, and Coverings.

The beautiful embroidered curtains were hid from all outside, by the goats' hair curtains which covered them completely. The beauties of those innermost set of curtains could only be viewed by the priests *in* the Tabernacle. Neither the curtains, nor the gold covered boards of the Tabernacle could be seen by an outsider. Then the goats' hair curtains were protected by the coverings of rams' skins, and the yet rougher material of the badger skin.

The exterior of the sacred edifice was in marked contrast to the interior. To anyone standing on the surrounding heights and looking down upon the Tabernacle standing within its court and protected on all sides, it must have had a mysterious significance. The utter absence of all pretension to beauty and ornament, so unlike the showy and even gorgeous temples of the heathen, must have struck the observer with surprise. What met the eye was the rough, coarse grained skin of the badger, which however effectually

protected the sacred building from external harm and injury.
Inside, the rough sands of the desert formed the floor of
God's dwelling, the sides were of purest gold, while the
hand-wrought, parti-coloured curtains with cherubic figures
embroidered in the pure white linen, formed the ceiling.

THE STORY THE CURTAINS UNFOLD.

What a story of Christ all this unfolds. The Tabernacle
both outside and inside, whether as viewed by an observer
without, or by a worshipper within, proclaimed the name and
worth of JESUS THE CHRIST AND SON OF GOD. These types
and shadows speak alone of Him ; otherwise all are meaningless.

" The fine *twined* linen " refers to the personal purity of
Christ ; His righteous character and absolute purity in
word, in life, in ways as shewn here on earth. The fine
linen in which the bride is adorned is said to be the
righteousness, or righteous acts of the saints (Rev. xix. 8).
In these the heavenly saints are adorned and clothed.
Righteousness and *Purity* are symbolised by the pure
linen : see Rev. xv. 6 ; Lev. xvi. 4.   The linen *fine twined*
would intimate that there was no sameness in the wondrous
life of Jesus. His life was one complete whole in which
every act and word had each its fitting place.   His
attributes, traits of character, and details of life, were
inseparably and harmoniously blended together.   Facts
and principles, character and life, were " twined " and
wrought into one whole : no discordant note or discord in
the music of that life which ever thrilled heaven, and above
all, the heart of God itself.

Then the colours wrought by hand in the linen contribute to these exquisite unfoldings of Christ. Why those special colours, and why ever in the same order—blue, purple, and scarlet? These colours in brief tell the history of Christ. In heaven (John iii. 13), yet as come from heaven (1 Cor. xv. 47), Christ ever bore the impress of heaven in all His life down here (*blue*). But He who came from heaven, suffered here as none other, and surely this is the symbolic meaning of the *purple* (Num. iv. 13). Then in a day not far distant, the glories and splendours of a redeemed world shall centre and circle round Him "Who is KING of kings and LORD of lords." "To Him shall be given of the gold of Sheba" (Ps. lxxii. 10-15), and of this the *scarlet* is the witness: see (Rev. xvii. 3-4: Lev. xiv. 6).

> "O the joy to see Thee reigning,
>   Thee my own beloved Lord;
> Every tongue Thy name confessing:
> Worship, honour, glory, blessing
>   Brought to Thee with one accord.
> Thee, my Master and my Friend,
>   Vindicated and enthroned,
> Unto earth's remotest end
>   Glorified, adored, and owned."

The purple is a combination of blue and scarlet. The purple speaks of the sufferings and death of One who came from heaven (the *blue*), and Who would step from the garden, the cross, and the sepulchre and mount to the throne and glory of the world (the *scarlet*) (Luke xxiv. 26).

The same combination of colours, in the same order, and proclaiming the same wondrous story of Christ, are written in the mystic veil, in the door of the tent, in the beautiful set of ten curtains, and in the gate of the court.

Cherubim* skilfully wrought in the three colours throughout the linen, shadowed forth the truth that the government of the world, as well as its glory (*scarlet*) is committed to Him Who alone is competent because of His Person, and alone worthy because of His work to sustain such a burden. The judicial authority of the Throne of the Eternal is to be publicly administered by the Son of Man (John v. 22-27).

The curtains must have been exceedingly beautiful. The highest skill, the finest and most exquisite needle-work, were lovingly and willingly spent on these curtains. *Christ* was imprinted on every fibre of the pure linen, on every colour, and on every cherubic figure. Ah! little did those generous and wise-hearted men and women of Israel know that in their work and labour of love, they were publishing to generations to come, the history of Christ— His wondrous Person, His offices, His suffering, His excellencies in life and death, and His coming glories.

THE ARRANGEMENT OF THE CURTAINS.

Their arrangement next demands attention. We have already remarked upon the dimensions of the curtains, each of the ten being twenty eight cubits in length, and four cubits in breadth. The ten were divided. Five were joined breadth to breadth, giving a total of twenty cubits in breadth. The other five were similiarly coupled together. Each five formed one curtain of twenty-eight cubits in length, and twenty cubits in breadth. Two curtains of exactly the same dimensions.

---

*Cherubim *plural*, Cherub *singular* ; Seraphim *plural*, Seraph *singular*.

Loops of blue "held one curtain to another" (xxxvi. 12). This reminds us of the truth of 1 Cor. xv. 48 the *heavenly One* in Whom and by Whom these Tabernacle-glories were united. There were in all 100 of these loops.

Then the two five-fold curtains were firmly united or bound together by 50 taches of gold-fastenings or clasps. It is generally thought that the taches were put through the loops but this is not said. The loops of blue knit the separate curtains together, while the gold taches or clasps coupled and secured in one the two five-fold curtains.

THE SYMBOLICAL MEANING OF THE MEASUREMENTS.

All this surely has a voice to us; every word of God is pure, and every word, and letter, and point inspired (Matt. v. 17-18). The *breath* of God* (2. Tim. iii. 15), and the *voice* of God (Heb. i. 2), are impressed on these undying records of God's Revelation of Himself.

> " A glory gilds the sacred page,
>   Majestic, like the sun :
> It gives a light to every age ;
>   It gives, but borrows none."

The linen directs us to the spotlessness of Christ in His humanity down here—holy and righteous. But why were the separate widths of the curtains each *four* cubits? Four is the numeral which speaks of the world—of the race at large: see Rev. vii. 9; Ezek. i. 5, 6, 8, 10. In the four cubits of linen, is embodied that magnificent

---

*Inspiration is applied to the Sacred Writings—composed of words and letters. The Scriptures are God-*breathed* such is the force and meaning of the word "inspiration."

declaration of John iv. 42, " This is indeed the Christ,
THE SAVIOUR OF THE WORLD "; just as the
four-square Brazen Altar points to His death for all (Heb.
ii. 9). The four cubits of linen is the Holy and Righteous
One, in His *life* towards the world (2 Cor. v. 19), and
the Brazen Altar His *death* for a guilty world. Both have
a universal bearing. The 28 cubits in length of the curtains
give four sevens. Seven the ruling number in the
Apocalypse, points to what is *morally complete* or *perfect,*＊
so the value of the two numerals, four and seven, which
enter into that of 28, would signify that Christ in His holy
life towards man, presents an unblemished, perfect life,
" Which of you convinceth me of sin " ? was the challenge
to the world then as now.

LOOPS OF BLUE AND TACHES OF GOLD.

The loops of blue—the colour of the firmament—which
held curtain to curtain, seem to teach that the *heavenly*
character of Christ—the Son of Man in heaven, even when
actually on the earth (John iii. 13, 31, 32)—bound up in
one all that Christ did and said. Christ's life here below
was the life of one Who belonged to heaven (John xiii. 3).
Then the taches or clasps of gold coupled in one (not the
separate curtains, one to another, that was the work of the
loops) the two five-fold curtains together. Ten signifies
responsibility towards *God*, five responsibility towards *man*.

＊*Seven* Kingdom-parables (Matt. xiii.). *Seven* Churches (Rev. ii. and iii.).
  Seven feasts of Jehovah (Lev. xxiii.). *Seven* seals (Rev. vi.). *Seven*
  horns (v.). *Seven* eyes (v.). *Seven* spirits of God (v.). The thought of
  what is *complete*, what is *perfect*, seems symbolised in this numeral of
  frequent occurrence.

But what maintained and secured intact the whole range and extent of human responsibility was *Divine righteousness*. Creature reponsibility has proved a complete failure, a universal break-down. The ten Commandments may be resolved under two heads : first responsibility to God, " thou shalt love the Lord thy God," second responsibility to man, thou shalt love " thy neighbour as thyself" (Luke x. 27). We have neither answered to the one nor to the other. The Lord has done both, and has made the law honourable in doing so. In Divine Righteousness He has met every demand, He has coupled in one great obedience, man's fullest responsibility on the Divine side, and on the human side as well. Intrinsic righteousness maintained all inviolate in the Divine Person, of our ever adorable Lord.*

The moral pillars of the universe are, RIGHTEOUSNESS and HOLINESS. These both meet in Christ. In the same Divine work God has been glorified, and our failed responsibility met in judgment to the utmost.

ONE TABERNACLE.

Now that the gold taches and loops of blue have coupled and secured all, the ten curtains in their marvellous story have become "*One* Tabernacle." It might be said, "there were two Tabernacles," for the Veil hung up under the taches, separated the holy from the holiest. "*One* Tabernacle" wraps up a mystery only explained when the Veil was rent (Matt. xxvii. 51), and thus the holy and

---

*We have responsibilities toward God—individual and corporate. We have each, too, responsibility towards the world, the Church, and to one another, and this latter must not be clouded or overshadowed by the former. Both must be preserved intact.

the holiest became manifestly " One " sanctuary, into which
all believers have equal, full, and free access (Heb. x. 19-22).
Nor is our entrance into the immediate presence of God
characterised by fear. The cross has done its mighty
work for God and in our consciences, and hence we draw
near in all holy boldness.

> " Eternal Light ! Eternal Light !
>   How pure the soul must be,
>   When, placed within Thy searching *sight*,
>   It shrinks not, but with calm delight
>   Can live, and look on Thee."

Thus the beautiful curtains in material, make, measure,
colours, and emblematic characters—united and secured in
one by loops of blue and clasps of gold—publish the whole
history of Christ in its great essential features, from heaven
(the *blue*), till the glory (*scarlet*), and the government of
the world (*Cherubim)* are borne by Him Who in His Person
and by His obedience and death, merits every glory and
honour of heaven and earth. Halleluiah what a Saviour !
The curtains over canopying and over shadowing the solid
structure, rest their weight on the gold covered boards, and
then tell their wonderful story to the worshippers within.
The binding, clasping, and uniting together of this truly
wonderful tale, entitles it to the appellation, " And the
Tabernacle shall be *one* " (Exod. xxvi. 6. R.V.)

HOW THE CURTAINS COVERED THE TABERNACLE-BOARDS.

The curtains were stretched lengthways across the
breadth of the Tabernacle—north to south. The width of
the sacred building was 10 cubits, and the height of the
boards on either side 10 cubits. Thus 30 cubits were
required to stretch across the breadth and cover the sides.

But the curtains being only 28 cubits, left one cubit of board exposed on either side. The goats' hair curtains however, supplied the deficency as they were each 30 cubits long, and thus completely covered over the exposed part of the boards on both sides.

Then the length of the Tabernacle 30 cubits, and the back or west end 10 cubits high, had to be provided for—40 cubits in all. The ten curtains, each four cubits in breadth give us 40 cubits, just what is required and no more. Thirty cubits the length of the sacred building and 10 cubits to hang down at the end, thus completely covering the west end boards.

THE IMPORTANCE OF THESE MEASUREMENTS.

It has been already remarked that the dividing Veil in the Tabernacle was hung up under the taches. Now as we have seen, there were 20 cubits of curtains on each side of these taches, under which the Veil was hung. This borne in mind enables us to fix with precision, the respective sizes of the holy and the most holy—the former being the sphere of *daily* ministration, and the latter of *yearly* service. The size of the holy place therefore, was 20 cubits long and 10 broad. The most holy, or, "holiest of all" was a square apartment 10 cubits by 10. We arrive at the result thus : The length of the Tabernacle was 30 cubits, and 10 cubits the height of the boards west. Now we have 40 cubits of curtains to cover up the Tabernacle in these two respects. But the 40 cubits were divided by the taches, 20 of which formed the length of the holy place, and 10 that of the holiest, the other 10 hanging over the west end boards. The breadth of the Tabernacle from north to south, was the same throughout—10 cubits.

The Goats' Hair Curtains.

(Exod. xxvi. 7-13; xxxvi. 14-18).

In almost every instance where we read "the *tabernacle* of the congregation," it should read "the *tent* of the congregation" (see R.V.). "Thou shalt make curtains of goats' hair * for a *tent* over the tabernacle"; again, "the forefront of the *tent*," *i.e.*, the goats' hair curtains. This was the only curtain which hung down at the front or east end.

The beautiful and embroidered tapestry, displaying in colour and Cherubim the highest skill in finest needlework, is termed the Tabernacle; over it was spread the Tent or goats' hair curtains; then the coverings of rams' skins dyed red, next badger or seal skins. Two sets of curtains and two coverings.

The Tent was made of 11 curtains, the Tabernacle of 10. The length of the Tent curtains was 30 cubits, the Tabernacle of 28 cubits. The breadth, four cubits, was the same in both Tabernacle and Tent curtains. The extra length of the goats' hair curtains—a cubit on each side—would not only cover the beautiful tapestry, but also the exposed part of the gold-covered boards on both sides. Thus no part of the beautiful embroidered curtains could be seen from the outside. Their beauties could only be discerned by those within. The moral beauties of the Lord can alone be witnessed in the sanctuary, and nowhere else. Intelligence, natural ability, keen perception are of no account here. The Holy Spirit can alone give eyes to see, ears to hear, and

---

* *Hair* is in italics, and is not found in the original. It was some very fine material, but not *hair*.

a heart to appreciate the moral perfections of Christ. His glories fill heaven and transport the inhabitants thereof.

> " O joy all joys beyond,
>   To see the Lamb Who died,
> And count each sacred wound
>   In hands, and feet, and side ;
> To give to Him the praise
>   Of every triumph won,
> And sing through endless days
>   The great things He hath done."

CHRIST IN LIFE AND DEATH.

The goat was pre-eminently the sin-offering (Lev. xvi. 5, 10). Thus in the deeply interesting ritual on the annual day of atonement, the sin-offerings took precedence of the burnt-offerings. Whereas in the normal order the burnt-offerings are first in historical sequence (see Lev. i. and iv.). The goats and sheep are contrasted : the former are sinners, the latter righteous persons (Matt. xxv. 32, 33). Christ was the great sin-offering. He poured out His soul unto death. His soul was made an offering for sin, hence of this sacrifice only it is said the priest "shall *pour* out all the blood thereof at the bottom of the Altar " (Lev. iv.). In the case of the burnt-offering the blood was sprinkled round about the altar (Lev. i.). *Poured* in the one, *sprinkled* in the other. But while the goat and sin are associated thoughts in the mind, it is Christ in life, and not on the Cross, which is before us in the goats' hair curtains, hence they point to Him as the Prophet of God, fulfilling His prophetic ministry here on earth, in absolute separation from evil.

> " His path, uncheered by earthly smiles,
>   Led only to the Cross."

The gorgeous tapestry within, and the rough exterior of the goat covering without, are thus set in sharp contrast. The outward severity of Christ's life in holy separateness from sin, thank God, not *from* sinners, would be the aspect towards man. Zech. xiii. 4 (margin) shews the import of what we are now considering. Christ, not actually as John (Matt. iii. 4), but *morally*, wore the prophetic mantle which necessarily kept Him apart from the sins of those whom He came to save, and this during His prophetic ministry on earth. But the Cross changed all. There He bore our sins and fulfilled His course on earth. We may remark that Heb. vii. 26 refers to Christ in heaven, not as down here. "Separate from sinners" should read "separated from sinners."

There was no beauty in this outer covering, and there was none in Christ that He should be desired. His visage was marred. There was neither beauty, form, nor comeliness in Him to fix the gaze and ravish the heart of an unbelieving world. It is in the sanctuary where the beauties and glories of Christ are disclosed. It is there that hearts are bowed and souls worship.

THE CURTAINS : THEIR DIVISION AND ARRANGEMENT.

" And thou shalt couple five curtains by themselves, and six curtains by themselves, and shalt double the sixth curtain in the forefront of the Tabernacle " (xxvi. 9).

There were eleven curtains in all. Five are coupled by themselves, width to width, namely, four cubits. The measurements were the same in all—30 cubits in length and four in breadth. Thus the six are coupled by themselves, not length to length, but breadth to breadth.

The sixth or additional curtain was to be doubled up in the east end or forefront of the Tabernacle. As the breadth was four cubits, it would, of course, expose two cubits of curtain when doubled. It is the same word that is used of the breastplate of the high priest: "Four-square it shall be, being *doubled*" (Exod. xxviii. 16). Into this pouch or bag were deposited "the Urim and the Thummim,* and they shall be upon Aaron's heart when he goeth in before the LORD" (verse 30). Thus to all observers in the Court two cubits of a goats' hair curtain met their gaze, and it is remarkable that no other curtains or coverings were allowed to hang down in the front, save this special one. This peculiar arrangement served a double purpose. It effectually screened from outside observation the golden hooks, golden chapiters—ornamental parts of the pillars – and the gold fillets or rods between the pillars, and on which were hung the hangings of the door. Thus these two cubits of doubled goats' hair were a continual witness to the condemnation of sin, and absolute separation from it by Christ, to Whom these curtains point.

"And the remnant that remaineth of the curtains of the tent, the half curtain that remaineth shall hang over the back side of the Tabernacle" (xxvi. 12). The meaning is that each of the five-fold curtains (the sixth measure was

---

* Urim and Thummim, supposed to be exceedingly precious and brilliant stones, literally signify *lights* and *perfections*. Enquiry was answered and difficulty solved as the light of the sanctuary was thrown on these stones. God's mind and will were thus revealed. God answered by Urim and Thummim.

doubled up at the entrance) was 20 cubits in breadth. The
first 20 therefore covered the Tabernacle up to the taches
under which hung the Veil; the second 20 cubits-breadth
covered the remaining part of the Tabernacle, namely, 10
cubits, the other 10 hung over the back at the west end,
completely covering the beautiful curtains from all outside.
Thus what hung over the back was a half curtain.

"And a cubit on the one side and a cubit on the other
side of that which remaineth in the length of the curtains
of the Tent, it shall hang over the sides of the Tabernacle
on this side, and on that side to cover it" (verse 13). The
Tabernacle curtains were each 28 cubits in length, which
when thrown over the boards left a cubit on each side—
south and north—exposed. But the goats' hair curtains,
being 30 cubits in length, thus completely covered the
sides. Thus the whole of the west end was covered, as
also the sides—no portion of the gold-covered boards could
be seen from the Court. These goats' hair curtains covered
all up from an outsider.

We may further remark that the *two* cubits of curtain
seen by all assembling in the Court (verse 9), intimate that
a *complete and sufficient testimony* was thus borne to Christ
in His prophetic ministry here below: for the force and
value of the numeral *two* see John viii. 17; Matt. xviii. 19;
Rev. xi. 3, 4, etc.

LOOPS AND TACHES.

The curtains were coupled by loops—of what material
or colour we know not—and by taches of brass. The
innermost curtains were secured by loops of *blue* and taches

of *gold*. Both gold and brass signify *Divine Righteousness*. The former metal is righteousness in God's presence— righteousness in its own intrinsic character; the latter, righteousness shewn in the judgment of evil according to the deserts of failed human responsibility.

The goats' hair curtains speak of Him in His rugged, severe, and solitary separation from all that was not of God, hence His withering exposure of hypocrisy and stern denunciations of sin (Matt. xxiii.). The taches of brass and loops would intimate that He the Holy and Righteous One was tested and tried. But His life in all its parts, in all His words and deeds, were knit together, secured in one. Righteousness coupled together the *manger* and the *cross*. Those taches of brass unite in one, God's love and God's wrath.

In the case of the goats' hair curtains the taches were put into the loops (xxvi. 11). This is not said of the Tabernacle curtains (verse 5). As the Tent curtains covered the Tabernacle ones, the brass taches must have been exactly over the gold taches, and underneath those the Veil was suspended. How intimate therefore the connection between righteousness in the Divine presence (the *gold* taches), and that same righteousness manifested on earth (the *brass* taches). The Divine and human meet in Christ.

SIN CONDEMNED IN THE LIFE AND IN THE DEATH OF CHRIST.

"For what the law could not do in that it was weak through the flesh, God sending His own Son in the likeness of sinful flesh, and for sin (or as a sacrifice for sin) condemned sin in the flesh " (Rom. viii. 3). Here we have two things—THE INCARNATION and THE CROSS. In both we have God's condemnation of sin. This was God's great lesson to Israel—to priests and people. It is God's supreme lesson to the Church in every age.

The sockets of *brass* on which rested securely the pillars supporting the door hangings, and the *goats'* hair above spoke of Christ. The hidden sockets as surely tell their tale, as the goats' hair seen by all. The former point to the Divine ability of Christ to sustain the judgment of God against sin. The latter also directs to Christ, but as the Prophet of God in His life of absolute separation from sin. The goats' hair seen by all in the Court, refer to sin condemned in the *Incarnation*, while the sockets of brass equally point us to the *Cross*, in which sin was judged and borne. There was no sin *on* Him and no sin *in* Him—all during His life (Num. xix. 2). On the Cross there were sins laid *on* Him, but never was sin *in* Him. There is no sin *on* us, but there is sin *in* us, and ever will be till death or the Coming part us and it for ever.

The curtains thus coupled and secured formed the Tent " that it may be *one* " (verse 11). The unity of office and glory centring in the Person of our Lord, seems expressed in verses 6 and 11—*one* Tabernacle and *one* Tent.

> " Not a sound invades the stillness,
>   Not a form invades the scene,
>   Save the voice of my Beloved,
>   And the Person of the King."

Rams' Skins Dyed Red.

(xxvi. 14 ; xxxvi. 19).

All that we can learn of this covering is told us in a couple of brief sentences.

The Tent covered the Tabernacle, then the rams' skins were placed over the Tent, while the outermost covering of all were the badgers' skins. The embroidered curtains *inside*, and the badgers' skins *outside!* The contrast is marked and spiritually deeply significant.

The Tabernacle and the Tent convey different, yet closely related ideas. The *Tabernacle* was where God dwelt and manifested Himself to the worshippers within. The displays of Christ were many and diversified. But the *Tent* signified the place where God could meet the people and address them through the Mediator. The priests inside — the Tabernacle. The people outside at the Tent door.

The rams' skins speak to us of Christ in His absolute consecration* to God. The ram was the consecration-sacrificial animal (Lev. viii. 22-29).

Two things were needed ere Aaron—Israel's first high priest—could enter upon his priestly work. He had to be anointed with oil and consecrated by blood. In both acts he is witnessed apart from his sons (Exod. xxix. 7 ; Lev. viii. 23). Aaron, as we have seen more than once, is a type of our Lord as the Christians' Great High Priest. Now

---

Consecration is not our act, but is effected in what God has done for us. *Consecrate*, literally, is to *fill the hand*, see margin of Exod. xxix. 9. The hand *filled* with all telling of Christ in His life and death (Lev. viii. 27).

Christ was anointed with the Holy Ghost (the *oil*) at His baptism (Acts x. 38), and consecrated by His own blood ere he could enter upon His priestly service in the heavenly sanctuary. Aaron was *not* high priest when anointed, or even when consecrated, but both were needful ere he could officially be recognised as such, so Christ was neither High Priest at His baptism, nor at any time when on earth. He had to be consecrated by His own blood. It was after both, *i.e.*, His life and death, that He entered upon His high priestly service in heaven. Christ could not be a Priest on this side of death, "for if He were on earth He should not be a Priest" (Heb. viii. 4).

Then Aaron's sons were consecrated. In the case of Aaron the oil was first applied, then the blood. But in that of the sons it was just the reverse order. *We* get the Spirit after, and consequent upon the blood being applied. Christ personally pure, was anointed by God with the Spirit—the Divine witness of His absolute purity and personal relation to the Father (Matt. iii. 16-17).

The tip of the right ear, thumb of the right hand, and the great toe of the right foot were each touched with blood; the whole man being thus set apart for God—hearing (ear), service (hand), and ways (foot)—were to be for Him alone. Now Aaron and his sons, in joint association, were thus consecrated. Aaron, as we have seen, was anointed and consecrated alone, as *also* his sons with him. So Christ and the whole priestly family are together in *one* consecration. He in the heavenly sanctuary for *us*, and we down here in service for *Him*.

The skins dyed *red* would express *absolute devotedness to God, even to death.*

This covering was not measured, nor were the badgers' skins, and in this respect these coverings are in marked contrast to the careful and repeated measurements of the Tabernacle and Tent curtains. The embroidered curtains within, signify Christ in relation to God and the heavenly priesthood; while Christ as outwardly witnessed by men in His prophetic service on earth—the rough goats' hair curtains. In both aspects He is infinitely precious to God, which seems the force of those two sets of curtains, *i.e.*, the Tabernacle and the Tent being measured. Measuring is God's special appropriation for Himself (Ezek. xl: Rev. xi: xxi). The outer coverings were not measured: they do not so directly present the Person of our Lord *to God:* while, of course, they convey truths about Him of profound importance *to us*.

In Num. iii. 25, we read that "the charge of the sons of Gershon in the tabernacle of the congregation shall be the *tabernacle,* and the *tent,* the *covering* thereof"; that is, the innermost set of curtains; then the goats' hair curtains, and over these the rams' skins dyed red. While in chap. iv. we have in one verse the respective curtains and coverings specified. "The curtains of the tabernacle (the *embroidered tapestry ones*), and the tent of the congregation (the *rough goats' hair curtains*), his covering (the *rams' skins dyed red*) and the covering of the *badgers' skins* that is above upon it" (verse 25).

Accepted, perfect, and complete
For God's inheritance made meet!
How true, how glorious, and how sweet."

Badgers' Skins.

(xxvi. 14 ; xxxvi. 19).

"Seal skins" is the reading in the revised version.
There may be some difficulty in determining the particular
animal meant, but the truth conveyed is the important
point. While a lengthened and detailed description of the
curtains are given, the coverings are simply named in a
couple of sentences. This covering is not measured. It
was put over all as a protection, so as to guard against
hostile influence without. This outer covering was imper-
vious to weather and climatic change. Neither the
scorching rays of the sun, nor the fiercest blast of storm
could reach Tent or Tabernacle. The whole was covered
up and effectually guarded and protected by this rough,
and tough material : see Ezek. xvi. 10.

All this points to our blessed Lord. No power of evil
without could reach His nature within. The temptations and
assaults of the enemy were powerless. He could say of
Himself, " Thou hast proved mine heart ; thou hast visited
me in the night ; thou hast tried me and shalt find nothing ;
I am purposed that my mouth shall not transgress. Concerning the works of men by the word of thy lips I have
kept me from the paths of the destroyer " (Ps. xvii. 3, 4).
Night and day vigilance, and holy separateness from all
outward evil characterised our Lord. He was proof against
evil *without*, and no touch of sin ever stained His nature
within. The beauties within were protected by this exterior
covering. The beauties and glories of heaven, are
maintained and upheld by the precious fact, that Christ
stood invulnerable amidst Satan's darts, wiles, and temptations. He ever stood firm as a rock.

Although not expressly stated we gather that the two coverings were spread over the whole Tabernacle—top, sides, and west end.

The suggested meanings of these curtains and coverings, are in keeping with the analogy of the faith, but are not *pressed* upon the acceptance of the reader. Symbolic and typical teaching must appeal to the spiritual instincts of believers, and of course, be in consonance with the broad lines of truth which are clearly revealed in the Sacred Word.

Dimensions of the Tabernacle and Temple.

The dimensions of the interior of the Tabernacle in length and breadth, so far exceeded by those of the Court is a surprise to many. We unthinkingly compare size of chapel and cathedral with the Tabernacle and Temple, but it is a mistake to do so. The Tabernacle without its Court, or the Temple without its Courts, could easily be accommodated within many of our modern chapels and cathedrals. The people congregated in the Court of the Tabernacle, while the priests alone could enter into the sanctuary, so too with the Temple. This latter had four Courts:

(1) The Court of the Gentiles.

(2) The Court of the women.

(3) The Court of Israel for the men.

(4) The Court of the priests.

But none of these were included in the Temple proper, into which the priests alone had the privilege of entrance. The priests *inside*. The people *outside*.

Christianity knows no such distinction. There is no material building on earth entitled to the designation, THE HOUSE OF GOD.* Judaism had its house of God, of stones, small, large, and costly—composed of *dead* material. Christianity has its house of God built up of *living* stones (1 Pet. ii. 5), and Christ the builder (Matt. xvi. 18). All such distinctions now as clergy and laity, priests and people, are utterly destitute of Divine authority. *All* the Lord's people are priests to God, and *all* have equal access to the heavenly sanctuary. In Judaism, however, the distinction between priests and people was a marked characteristic of that dispensation. The Tabernacle was small in comparison with the Court, but quite large enough for the fullest priestly service required. Probably but one priest at a time ministered in the Tabernacle. It was so at least on the yearly day of atonement (Lev. xvi. 17).

---

*Besides the Tabernacle, there are five material Temples spoken of in the Scriptures—three are things of the past, two are future. *First*, Solomon's Temple destroyed by the Chaldeans a month after the sack and capture of Jerusalem (2 Kings xxv.). *Second*, Zerubbabel's Temple which had not the distinguishing presence of God (the Ark), nor His manifested glory (the sheckinah or glory cloud between the cherubim). *Third*, Herod's Temple larger by far than Solomon's; forty-six years in building (John ii. 20), and destroyed by the Romans in the year 70 A.D. *Fourth*, yet future, Antichrist's Temple built by restored Judah in unbelief, to be destroyed by the Antagonist of the Jewish people, the Assyrian or King of the North (Ps. lxxiv; lxxix.). *Fifth*, Christ's millennial Temple which He will personally enter (Ezek. xl.).

The following table will give a correct idea of the relative size of the interior of the Tabernacle and of the Temples:—

	Length from East to West.	Width from North to South.	Height of the Interior.
The Tabernacle, - -	30 cubits.	10 cubits.	The height
Solomon's Temple, -	70 cubits.	20 cubits.	differed from
Zerubbabel's Temple,	70 cubits.	60 cubits.	10 cubits
Herod's Temple, - -	100 cubits.	70 cubits.	to 60 cubits.*

The Tabernacle was divided by the Veil into two unequal apartments. The *first* was the Sanctuary or Holy Place, being 20 cubits or 30 feet in length, 10 cubits or 15 feet in breadth, and 10 cubits or 15 feet in height. The *second* was the Oracle or Holy of Holies, which was a square apartment, being 10 cubits in length, width, and height. It will thus be seen that not more probably, than one person could officiate at the same moment.

It is important to bear in mind that neither the size nor costly adornments of Tabernacle and Temple, constituted them objects of surpassing national interest. It was the presence and glory of Jehovah which made *that*—in itself relatively small—great beyond all else in comparison.

WITHIN.

No natural or artificial light penetrated into the Holiest. The sheckinah was its only light, and all outside its searching rays was thick darkness. The sanctuary had its seven-

---

* "The reductions of the dimensions to English feet is approximately determined by the Siloam inscription, which gives a round number of 1200 cubits for a measured length of 1760 feet. The Hebrew cubit, therefore, was the short cubit of antiquity, and for practical purposes may be taken as equal to the Greek cubit of 18 inches, used by Josephus for the measurements of Herod's temple."
—*Encyclopædia Britannica*—Article *Temple.*

branched golden Candlestick which burned all night. The import of this we shall consider when we come to examine the vessels within.

How resplendent! Inside, the walls on both sides a sight of purest gold; above, the beautiful tapestry—a gorgeous mass of colour and cherubim; right in front of the Veil stands the golden Incense Altar, and on either side the golden Candlestick and golden Table of Shewbread, or "Exhibition bread"; facing the priest was the Veil, and behind him the door. But what was beneath his feet? The sand of the desert. But above all is the grand fact: God on His throne is *within*. He sanctified the Tabernacle with His glory.

> " O who that glorious blaze
> Of living light shall tell,
> Where all His brightness God displays,
> And the Lamb's glories dwell?
>
> God and the Lamb shall there
> The Light and Temple be,
> And radiant hosts for ever share
> The unveiled mystery."

The Tabernacle : Inside.

The words Tabernacle and Tent are each applied to the sacred enclosure we are about to enter. The former signifies that it was God's dwelling; the latter the place where God met His people. Then, as we have seen, the two sets of curtains were respectively denominated the Tabernacle (the innermost curtains) and the Tent (the goats' hair curtains).

As priests we enter—only as sinners saved by sovereign grace we pass through the Veil into the heavenly sanctuary. None but Aaron, his sons, and Moses the Mediator could minister in the holy place. Silence reigned in the sacred apartment. No prayer was offered, no song was sung. The voice of man was hushed, but the voice of those vessels of gold mutely, yet eloquently, spoke of Christ. Constant daily service—never ceasing, never ending before that unrent Veil for 500 years, told a mournful tale of imperfect service and sin-burdened consciences. God was hid behind the beautiful Veil. *When* will it be rent or removed? *When* will a sinful creature be able to stand holily and righteously before the Throne of Jehovah, and have its full blaze of glory search Him through and through? *When* will sinners be brought face to face with God Himself, and made divinely fit to gaze in love and holy fear on the uncreated glory of God in the face of Jesus?

THE ALL-SUFFICIENT SACRIFICE.

Not till a sacrifice is offered which will satisfy God in respect to sin, cleanse the guilty conscience, and save the vilest sinner believing on Jesus. That sacrifice has been offered to God, and accepted by Him. The Altar of old was ever and ever demanding fresh sacrifice. The fire was never satisfied. Now we *know* of a sacrifice of infinite value which has consumed the fire, and it burns *no more*. Hallelujah! it is done. The Veil was rent, not removed, by the hand of God, "rent in the midst" (Luke xxiii. 45), and "from the top to the bottom" (Matt. xxvii. 51). Now in faith and in the power of the Holy Ghost, we pass through the rent Veil into the innermost sanctuary, the *immediate* presence of God (Heb. x. 19). It is all God's presence now.

No temple in heaven, and no dividing Veil separating God from the worshippers. Believers have been brought, not near to God, but *to God* Himself in all the majesty of His Being, and in all the love of His nature. *Who* has done this? God. *What* has done this? THE BLOOD OF JESUS. Let it be written in letters of gold that our only trust in time and eternity, in earth and heaven, is THE PRECIOUS BLOOD OF CHRIST.

> " The balm of life, the cure of woe,
>   The measure and the pledge of love ;
>   The sinner's refuge here below,
>   The angels' theme in heaven above."

We do not cower or fear, as with unsandalled feet we tread the heavenly Courts. The blood of Jesus imparts " boldness," yet rebukes presumption. For us, then, the Veil *is* rent; of old it stood as a barrier to the further approach of the most holy of Israel's priesthood. None but the High Priest could enter that most sacred spot on earth—only once a year, and then not without incense and blood.* Our Altar is the Cross. Our place of worship is the heavenly sanctuary. Our Great High Priest is above. The Holy Spirit is our power for worship. Our sacrifices are praise to God and practical benevolence to the needy, and God Himself has become the object of our worship.

RITUALISM.

The only ritualistic system of Divine authority was the one set up in the midst of Israel. That *morally* ceased

---

* The entrance of Moses the Mediator, who, as such, was not under the law, could, in virtue of his office, enter the sanctuary apart from blood (Num. vii. 89 ; Lev. i. 1). As a man, he needed the blood as any one else, but not as Mediator. It was Aaron, however, who represented the people before God, hence he must come with blood and by it.

when the Lord of the temple bowed His head in death—
God's sacrificial Lamb for the sin of the world. *Historically*,
it was closed up in judgment when the Roman ploughshare
passed over Zion in the year 70 A.D. Ritualism is perpetua-
tion of shadow. It denies *in toto* the Christianity of the
New Testament, and is an affront to the glory of God. Its fate
is as sure as that inflicted on apostate Judaism by the sword
of the Roman. God Himself set up a system of Ritualism on
earth, which after having served its purpose He destroyed.
He will set up another in millennial times (Ezek. xl.-xlviii.)—
a *commemorative* system, as the former was *anticipative*.
But between these—past and present systems—Christianity
in its doctrine and history comes in; its living power being
the Holy Ghost. In these 2000 years between the past and
future of Israel, there is neither need nor room for Ritualism.
What a travesty of the elaborate and burdensome system
established by God in Israel, in modern altars, candles,
crosses, petticoated priests, and all the silly mummery and
paraphernalia of modern Ritualism, more fit to be regarded
as a show for children than to be termed worship. Contempt
for these geegaws is our feeling. Pity for the deluded
devotees—*Worshippers* shall we term them?—only such in
name and form.

> " What wonders in my Saviour meet !
>   His head, His hands, His side, His feet
> Present to my astonished view
>   Eternal glories, ever new."

> "Here all the ancient types agree,
>   The altar and the Lamb ;
> And prophets in their vision see
>   Salvation through His name."

The Altar of Incense ; or Golden Altar.
(xxx. 1-10).

"And thou shalt make an altar to burn incense upon : of shittim wood shalt thou make it.

"A cubit shall be the length thereof, and a cubit the breadth thereof ; foursquare shall it be : and two cubits shall be the height thereof : the horns thereof shall be of the same.

"And thou shalt overlay it with pure gold, the top thereof, and the sides thereof round about, and the horns thereof, and thou shalt make unto it a crown of gold round about.

"And two golden rings shalt thou make to it under the crown of it, by the two corners thereof, upon the two sides of it shalt thou make it ; and they shall be for places for the staves to bear it withal.

"And thou shalt make the staves of shittim wood, and overlay them with gold.

"And thou shalt put it before the veil that is by the ark of the testimony, before the mercy-seat that is over the testimony, where I will meet with thee.

"And Aaron shall burn thereon sweet incense every morning : when he dresseth the lamps he shall burn incense upon it.

"And when Aaron lighteth the lamps at even, he shall burn incense upon it ; a perpetual incense before the LORD throughout your generations.

"Ye shall offer no strange incense thereon, nor burnt sacrifice, nor meat offering ; neither shall ye pour drink offering thereon.

"And Aaron shall make an atonement upon the horns of it once in a year with the blood of the sin-offering of atonements: once in the year shall he make atonement upon it throughout your generations: it is most holy unto the LORD."

We have already remarked upon the omission of the Golden Altar and Brazen Laver in the account from their respective places in the Holy and in the Court (xxv.; xxvii.). The sacred historian takes no notice of those two vessels in the general description already given us; they are "vessels of approach," not "vessels of display"; that is, they refer to our intercourse with God—our presentation to Him where He is. Those already so fully and minutely described, set forth the great and fundamental truth of God's manifestation of Himself to man (xxv.-xxvii. 19). But God's revelation of Himself, had in view the direct object of our being brought to God, hence the priesthood, the Golden or Incense Altar, and the Laver were needful if this great purpose was to be attained. While the Brazen Altar was the ground or moral basis of our approach to God, the means were the Golden Altar (in figure) expressive of our worship and communion, the Brazen Laver for practical cleansing and holiness in view of our drawing nigh to God, and a living priesthood to introduce us into the Divine presence and uphold our interests there. Christ does all this *for* us, and He is all this *to* us. He is Priest, Golden Altar, and Brazen Laver.*

The Incense Altar is named before the other priestly vessel—the Laver—because access to God in the sanctuary derived all its force and value from the Altar in the Court without. It is in the value of the Brazen Altar

---

* From the Ark inside till the Altar outside, it is God manifesting Himself; whereas we travel from the Altar to the Ark. From God to man is the Divine order; from man to God is the human order, and one based moreover on our exceeding need.

that we are placed in *immediate* connection with God where He is. The Laver was for *practical* cleansing. The two altars—the one without and the other within—exhibit a moral connection. There could be no worship at the *Golden* Altar had there not been sacrifice on the *Brazen* Altar. First, sacrifice; then worship. All worship, however elaborate the machinery, is mere ritual and even worse, an abomination to the LORD, where it is not directly based upon, and derives all its value from the one offering of Christ on the Cross to God. In the value of the Brazen Altar we are set beside the Golden Altar as worshippers; such is the worth of the infinite sacrifice of Christ. Sacrifice and worship are inseparable, and of this chaps. ix. and x. of the Epistle to the Hebrews are the witness.

DIMENSIONS, SHAPE, MATERIAL, AND PLACE OF THE ALTAR.

Dimensions.—The Golden Altar was foursquare. The Brazen Altar, too, was foursquare. Both altars faced the world—north, south, east, and west. The Golden Altar of Incense was two cubits in height, and only half that in length and breadth, namely, one cubit. It may be interesting to compare the dimensions of the holy vessels. In reducing the cubits to English measurements, we adopt the computation of Josephus, who regarded the cubit as about 18 inches.

VESSELS.	HEIGHT.	LENGTH.	BREADTH.
GOLDEN ALTAR, - -	36 inches.	18 inches.	18 inches.
BRAZEN ALTAR, - -	4 feet, 6 ins.	7 feet, 6 ins.	7 feet, 6 ins.
TABLE OF SHEWBREAD,	27 inches.	36 inches.	18 inches.
THE ARK, - - - -	27 inches.	3 feet, 9 ins.	27 inches.
MERCY-SEAT, - - -	Not given.	3 feet, 9 ins.	27 inches.

GOLDEN CANDLESTICK—*unmeasured.*
BRAZEN LAVER—*unmeasured.*

The height of the Mercy-seat is not given, being included in that of the Ark, of which it formed an integral part; yet they can be separately regarded. The two Altars are each said to be foursquare.

Materials of which the Altar was made were shittim wood and gold, surely pointing to Christ in the combined glory of His Person—INCORRUPTIBLE HUMANITY and ABSOLUTE DEITY. It was all covered over with pure gold—none of the wood could be seen. The same materials—wood and gold—entered into the construction of the Ark and Table of Shew-bread. Shittim-wood and brass formed the Brazen Altar; gold alone in the Mercy-seat and Candlestick, and brass alone in the Laver. The union of the shittim-wood and gold point to that distinguished and *vital* truth of Christianity, *God* manifest in the *flesh*—GOD in holy humanity in the manger—GOD in wearied yet perfect human nature at the Well of Sychar—GOD in suffering humanity agonizing in the Garden—and, marvel of all wonders, GOD in a humanity unstained for 33 years bore on the Cross our sins and Divine judgment also.

"Thou shalt make upon it a crown of gold round about" (verse 11). This statement is a finger-post directing us to *that* sight. "We see Jesus, who was made a little lower than the angels for the suffering of death, *crowned with glory and honour*" (Heb. ii. 9). Jesus in heaven is both our Priest and incense or Golden Altar. We worship there—the heavens are the sphere of worship.

There is a vital connection between the two Altars. Both have horns; both have rings and staves. The horns of the Brazen Altar constitute the strength and protection of any guilty *sinner* laying hold of them. The horns of the Golden

Altar are the strength and refuge of the weakest *saint*. The journeying character of both Altars is intimated in the staves and rings; for while the Brazen Altar is for the *world* at large, the Golden Altar is for the *Church* at large. In the latter the rings were gold and the staves gold covered; in the other the rings were brass and the staves brass covered.

The *position* of the Altar in the Holy Place is interesting. It was placed right in front of the beautiful Veil. On the south side or left hand stood the seven-branched Golden Candlestick, while on the north side or right hand stood the Table of Shewbread. The general position may be indicated thus:—

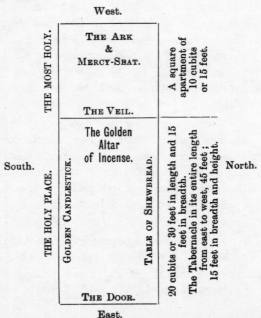

West.

THE MOST HOLY.

THE ARK & MERCY-SEAT.

A square apartment of 10 cubits or 15 feet.

THE VEIL.

The Golden Altar of Incense.

South.

THE HOLY PLACE.

GOLDEN CANDLESTICK.

TABLE OF SHEWBREAD.

20 cubits or 30 feet in length and 15 feet in breadth. The Tabernacle in its entire length from east to west, 45 feet; 15 feet in breadth and height.

North.

THE DOOR.

East.

The position of the Altar in front of the Veil has surely its significance—the two are morally connected. There could not be worship in heaven till the Veil was rent, and God revealed in the glory of His nature. The connection of the Altar with the Veil, Ark, and Mercy-seat is of deepest spiritual interest (verse 6).

"And Aaron shall burn thereon sweet incense (or incense of spices) every morning: when he dresseth the lamps, he shall burn incense upon it. And when Aaron lighteth the lamps at even he shall burn incense upon it: a *perpetual incense* before the LORD throughout your generations."

Much of the Jewish ritual is inexplicable unless the association of Aaron and his sons are kept in view. Not every ordained priest could do *high* priestly work. The office of the high priest and his pre-eminent place in the Jewish ecomony were unique. Aaron alone could make atonement. He alone of the nation was privileged to enter the holiest of all. Aaron alone dared part the Veil and enter into the awful presence of Jehovah bearing the judgment of Israel on his shoulders and on his heart (Exod. xxviii. 12, 29).[*] Aaron alone could wear the golden plate upon the mitre engraved with—

HOLINESS TO THE LORD.

---

[*]Aaron, we suppose, never did enter the holiest in his robes of glory and beauty. The sin of his sons was the immediate cause of the prohibition not to enter within the Veil, save by blood and incense yearly, and then in linen garments. But the high priests' pontifical attire (Exod. xxviii.) has its answer in Christ now and in millennial days. He serves in the heavenly sanctuary after the pattern of Aaron. In the coming day He acts in the combined character of Priest and King—after the pattern of Melchizedek (Zech. vi. 13).

Hence for these and other services Aaron was anointed, consecrated, and clothed apart from his sons. The Levites were debarred from the priesthood, but the priests were equally forbidden to usurp the functions and office of the high priest. While all this is true and should be insisted upon, it is equally important to view Aaron in his official appointment and service as identified with his sons. "And thou shalt put them (the priestly garments) upon Aaron and his sons *with him*: and shall anoint *them*, and consecrate *them*, and sanctify *them* that they may minister unto me in the priest's office—and they shall be upon Aaron and upon his sons when they come in unto the tabernacle of the congregation or when they come near unto the Altar to minister in the holy place" (Exod. xxviii. 41-43).

The identification of Aaron with his sons prefigures our association with Christ our Great Priest in the heavenly sanctuary. It is there where He intercedes; it is there where we worship. He sings (Heb. ii. 12); we sing (Rev. v.). He sustains and leads our worship. His powerful and ever prevailing intercession secures us all help by the way, all succour in need. The failure in our priestly service is met by His intercessional grace. He is our incense Altar.

Aaron burned incense on the Altar when he *lit* the lamps and when he *dressed* them. Christ in all the value and moral glories of His Person fills heaven with fragrance. He is the *perpetual* incense ever burning on the Golden Altar. But we too have a place at *that* Altar. We too burn incense in the presence of our God. We extol the merits of Jesus God's Beloved Son. His name, His glories, His excellencies; what He was and did, what He is and doing, what He shall be and do; His suffering in the past, His exaltation now, and His yet future triumphs and glories form the material of our worship in heaven itself. But for this the lamps must be lit, and this our heavenly Aaron does for each worshipper. He is light and He was the light of the world. We are light in the Lord, and " Ye are the light of the world "—all believers are such. *He* has made us this. But He also dresses and trims the lamps and supplies the oil (the Holy Spirit) to keep it burning. The moral connection between the light and worship is thus apparent. It is only those who *shine* that can *worship*. A dimmed light gives feeble worship. Shine well and you will worship well.

THE INCENSE : ITS COMPOSITION.

The incense was compounded of four precious ingredients (xxx. 34-38). It was a pure and holy perfume being prepared after a Divine formula, and not to be compounded for any other purpose under pain of death. It was a special incense. Those sweet spices, Stacte, Onycha, Galbanum—of which almost nothing is known—with "pure frankincense " in equal proportions were carefully tempered together, and this compound formed the delightful perfume which filled the holy place with its exquisite fragrance. Each of the four ingredients had its own peculiar aroma, but when all were blended they formed but one perfume. This then was burned on the Altar morning and night. It was thus a *perpetual* incense. Is there ever an hour—night or day—when the moral perfections and beauties of Christ do not fill heaven with their fragrance? The worthiness of Christ is proclaimed in song and story—by men and angels—now and ever (Rev. v.).   But *how* was the aroma extracted from these spices?   The secret is disclosed in Lev. xvi. 12, 13. The tempered incense was beaten small, and then thrown on the pan or censer of burning coals taken from off the Brazen or Judgment Altar.   It was the fire which consumed the sacrifice that brought forth the delightful aroma of the incense. It was Calvary which brought out the perfections of Christ. It was there that those deep and inward glories and excellencies of His nature and Person burst their channels and broke out in that very hour when for sin and in the place of sin He died.   How otherwise could His perfections have been exhibited?   These glories—profound and moral—fill heaven as "a perpetual incense."   The more searching the judgment, the deeper and richer the fragrance of what He was and what He did.   The more certain flowers are crushed and pressed, the richer the aroma.

On this Altar of Gold "no strange incense" was to be laid : see Lev. x. 1, 2. Jehovah's incense must be prepared according to His command and no "strange fire" must be used—it *must* be that taken from the Altar in the Court, *i.e.* the Cross.   Nor was sacrifice to be offered thereon, or any drink offering to be poured on it (verse 9). Blood never stained the Incense Altar except on the yearly day of atonement.   All the service in worship and in burning incense—unceasing daily service throughout the year—must rest on the ground of atonement made by blood; to this Lev. xvi. 18 refers. The moral efficacy of the Golden Altar rests on the blood of atonement : see Exod xxx.

10 with Lev. xvi. 18; the latter is the accomplishment of the former.

The evening and morning sacrifice on the Brazen Altar, the evening and morning burning of incense on the Golden Altar, the evening and morning lighting and dressing the lamps of the Golden Candlestick, and the evening and morning time of prayer were coincident actions. The moral connection of those things and their direct relation to Christ, might well form a delightful study and ground of many a profitable hour of thought. Read over carefully the following passages Exod. xxvii. 21; xxix. 38, 39; xxx. 7, 8; Ps. cxli. 1, 2; Luke i. 9, 10.

We may remark that the prayers—especially of suffering saints—are as incense to God (Rev. v. 8). But what makes their prayers, their groans, their worship so precious to Him is not in anything derived from themselves, but solely in the merits of another. The Angel-Priest gives value to our prayers and intercessions by adding His incense to them. His personal efficacy is our worth and value before God (Rev. viii. 3). Christ in heaven is our Golden Altar. The merits of His Person our incense. "By Him we offer the sacrifice of praise to God continually."

The Altar in its wood, gold, crown, rings, staves, and sweet incense of precious ingredients, speaks of Christ in His Being, in the mystery of His Person, of His travels with His people, and of His moral grace and beauties, sustaining and giving character to our worship before God. The connection, too, on which we have already remarked, between the Altar *within* for worship, and the Altar *without* expressive of judgment, is seen in the fact so precious and touching to us, that it was fire from the judgment Altar, which brought out the perfume of the incense at the worship Altar. In us trials manifest dross. In Christ the fire manifested His moral beauty and perfectness.

The Altar in preparation for its journeys was first covered over with a cloth of blue. It was essentially a heavenly vessel, and hence heaven's own colour wrapped it up, over that was spread a covering of badger's skins, thus effectually protecting it from outward defilement or hurt (Num. iv. 11). What befel the golden Altar when Solomon's temple was erected we know not. The Temple Altar was made of *Cedar* and gold (1 Kings vi. 20). The Tabernacle Altar was constructed of *Shittim* wood and gold (Exod. xxx. 1-3). It was on the right side of the Golden Altar that Gabriel stood and appeared to Zecharias in announcing the birth of the baptist (Luke i). There is no special mention of this Altar in the Temple spoils taken by Titus in the conclusion of the ever memorable siege of Jerusalem. We may remark in closing, that this Altar was exclusively employed for the burning of incense. The annual day of atonement was an exception, then not incense, but blood was seen on the Altar and on its horns—blood on the gold—and why? because the sin of the priest reached unto and defiled the Golden Altar (Lev. iv. 7). One interesting distinction meets us here. The sin of a priest or of the whole congregation, interrupted the communion of the people with Jehovah which was carried on at the Golden Altar, hence blood was put upon its horns only, not upon the Altar itself. But a year's service at the Altar carried many imperfections with it, hence an annual sprinkling of the blood upon the Altar itself and on its horns as well. Our worship is based on atonement. For us, too, the "ONE OFFERING" has set us down in God's presence in light and in cloudless peace and acceptance.

> " Oh, worship the King, all glorious above ;
>   Oh, gratefully sing His power and His love :
> Our Shield and Defender, the Ancient of Days,
>   Pavilioned in splendour, and girded with praise.

> O measureless might ! Ineffable love !
>   While angels delight to praise Thee above,
> The humbler creation, though feeble their lays,
>   With true adoration shall sing to Thy praise."

The Golden Candlestick.

"And thou shalt make a candlestick of pure gold : of beaten work shall the candlestick be made ; his shaft, and his branches, his bowls, his knops, and his flowers shall be of the same.

"And six branches shall come out of the sides of it : three branches of the candlestick out of the one side, and three branches of the candlestick out of the other side.

"Three bowls made like unto almonds, with a knop and a flower in one branch : and three bowls made like almonds in the other branch with a knop and a flower : so in the six branches that come out of the candlestick.

" And in the candlestick shall be four bowls made like unto almonds, with their knops and their flowers.

" And there shall be a knop under two branches of the same, and a knop under two branches of the same, and a knop under two branches of the same according to the six branches that proceed out of the candlestick.

" Their knops and their branches shall be of the same : all it shall be one beaten work of pure gold.

" And thou shalt make the seven lamps thereof : and they shall light the lamps thereof, that they may give light over against it.

" And the tongs thereof, and the snuff dishes thereof shall be of pure gold.

" Of a talent of pure gold shall he make it, with all these vessels.

" And look that thou make them after their pattern, which was showed thee in the mount" (Exod. xxv. 31-40).

PURE OIL OLIVE FOR THE LAMPS.

" And the Lord spake unto Moses, saying, " Command the children of Israel, that they bring unto thee pure oil olive beaten for the light, to cause the lamps to burn continually.

" Without the vail of the testimony in the Tabernacle of the congregation, shall Aaron order it from the evening unto the morning before the LORD continually : it shall be a statute for ever in your generations.

" He shall order the lamps upon the pure candlestick before the LORD continually " (Lev. xxiv. 1-4).

The Candlestick of pure gold, and the pure oil olive next demand our consideration. The Candelabrum stood in the south side of the holy place, and the Table of Shewbread exactly opposite. The only other vessel in the sacred apartment was the Incense Altar which stood right in front of the Veil.

There were no windows in the Tabernacle, no created light as the sun, no borrowed light as the moon, no artificial light as the candle illumined the holiest of all. There you are in the region of the Divine. "God is light." The holiest was lighted up by the glory cloud between the cherubim, while the holy place must have been a blaze of brilliant light from the seven branched Golden Candlestick. Neither was there a chimney nor aperture of any sort by which the burning incense could escape. The sacred perfume which had its strength and fragrance drawn out by the fire of the Brazen Altar, filled the holy place constantly, and the holiest once a year. The light and the perfume were for those *within*.

THE SPIRITUAL SIGNIFICATION OF THE CANDLESTICK.

The Candelabrum is Christ. The oil is the Spirit. The Candlestick was made wholly of the most precious of metals, pure gold, no shittim or other wood being employed in its construction. The Candlestick was wholly of gold; the Laver was entirely of brass. There were no measures nor dimensions of either. Both vessels represent Christ. The former had its place and use *inside*; the latter had its place and use *outside*.

Christ as man on earth was "the light" (John i. 7-9). "the light of men" (verse 4); and "the light of the world"

(viii. 12). But the incarnation, that is, God manifest in flesh, neither created life nor light, but manifested both—revealed to men what previously existed. " God is light," and it is in this sense that we view the Candlestick—Christ in His Divine nature as the light of all heaven.

We are privileged to take Christ's place in the world as its one and only light. We are " the light of the world " (Matt. v. 12). The seven *separate* Candlesticks or Lampstands of the Apocalypse (i. 20) are to light up the dense moral darkness prevailing on every hand. " The seven candlesticks *are* the seven churches." Need we say that all light, moral or physical, is derived from Him who is its source and fountain. The tiniest star-twinkler does so in virtue of Him.

But Christ was and ever shall be the light, is not exactly the truth conveyed in the Golden Candlestick in the holy place. It is the acacia wood which sets forth the incorruptible humanity of our Lord, and the white linen the holy life and righteous character of the One born of the virgin.* But in the pure Gold Candlestick, as also in the Mercy-seat entirely of gold, we have prefigured what is Divine. It is Divine light in the sanctuary in the power of the Holy Ghost. But in Whom and by Whom is the light expressed. In the heavenly City beheld by the Seer of Patmos we read "the glory of God did lighten it, and the Lamb is the light (rather *lamp*) thereof." It is the Lamb which transmits the rays of the Divine glory throughout heaven, and the future city of gold as well. Christ is the sevenfold light of the sanctuary.

---

*Isa. vii. 14 and Matt. i. 23 should read "*the* virgin," Luke i. 27 "*a* virgin."

It is light in all its innate purity which is shadowed forth by the pure gold in which there was no alloy. The pure oil* of special preparation could only be poured into pure gold bowls of unique description. Both the gold and the oil were beaten.

THE CONSTRUCTION OF THE CANDELABRUM.

The Candlestick and its dishes were made out of a talent of pure gold—about 125 pounds weight, The gold employed was of the finest and purest procurable; supposed to be in value of about 6000 pounds ·sterling.†

The Candelabrum consists of (1) the shaft on which the centre branch rested; (2) the upright massive column termed "his branch" (xxxvii. 17); (3) six branches—three on either side; (4) the bowls to receive the oil‡; (5) knops for ornament; (6) flowers for beauty; with the accessories (7) snuffers or tongs; (8) snuff-dishes to receive the waste or snuffings. In addition to all these we read, "and thou shalt make the seven lamps thereof" (xxv. 37). These lamps were put on the extremities of the branches including the massive centre one.

---

*The *oil* figures the Holy Spirit Matt. xxv. 4 ; 1 John ii. 20 ; 2 Cor. i. 21.

†In Solomon's Temple there were ten such (1 Kings vii. 49, 50). In Herod's Temple there seems to have been only one Candlestick as in the Tabernacle. It was carried away amongst other spoils by Titus in the plunder and destruction of Jerusalem, and graced his triumphal procession into Rome. When Genseric early in the fifth century sacked Rome he took the candlestick with him to Carthage. From thence it was brought to Constantinople, then back again to Jerusalem. It *may* be in existence but what became of it is not known.

‡ See Zech. iv. Bowl or basin to hold the oil, then pipes conveying it to the lamps.

But a few further details are added. On each of the six branches there were displayed three bowls—a bowl, a knop, and a flower alternately (xxv. 33); while in the Candlestick (verse 34), *i.e.*, the centre branch were four bowls with knop and flower—a bowl, a knop, and a flower alternately. Besides, there was a knop under each two branches—three in all. Those three knops must have hung across the upright branch—from the side branch to the other side branch, probably in the shape of a pendant. All were hammered into shape and beauty. The massive centre piece with its ornaments and flowers, must have presented a magnificent and valuable piece of workmanship.

THE THREEFOLD OBJECT OF THE CANDLESTICK.

The sevenfold light of the Candlestick was first to light up the interior of the holy place. All other light was excluded. The gold on the sides, and the beautiful curtains above, could only have their glories and beauties witnessed in the light. The light brought out imperfections, if such existed. The exquisite beauties of the holy place—above and around—were discovered by the light.

The second purpose of the lamps was to give light over against the Candlestick (xxv. 37). "When thou lightest the lamps the seven lamps shall give light over against the candlestick. And Aaron did so, he lighted the lamps over against the candlestick" (Num. viii. 2-3).

The beauties of the Candlestick, its purity of gold, its ornamental work, its flowers, its exquisite blending of bowl, knop, and flower on its branches and stem, the wonderful workmanship of the whole could only shine in the light: otherwise these glories were hid. God has put the beauties of His Son upon us. His moral likeness is what the Spirit would exhibit in each of us. By and bye we shall wake up with His likeness stamped on the sinless brow. The light of the Spirit is to discover the beauties of Christ. In the Son these perfections and glories shine forth in the sanctuary in Divine effulgence. In us down here the gold snuffers have to be often used, never so with Him. He is the Golden Candelabrum, the absolute reflector of the light of God—no flaw, no dimmed glory in Him. Absolute and alone in His beauty, perfection, and glory.

The third purpose to be served by the lamps was to throw their combined light on the table of Shew-bread. The Candlestick and the Table were placed exactly opposite each other (xxvi. 35; xii. 24). The Candlestick was "put in the tent of the congregation, over against the table on the side of the tabernacle southward." Light and food in the holy place. It was so then, it is so now. There were *twelve* loaves on the Table, and *seven* lights in the Candlestick. The former numeral refers to RULE and GOVERNMENT in connection with Israel in millennial days (Matt. xix. 28; Rev. xii. 1): the latter number expresses what is SPIRITUALLY COMPLETE (Rev. v. 6). The teaching therefore is of great value as opening up the present and future in relation to the whole nation of Israel. The twelve tribes are represented by the twelve loaves on the Table; believers of this dispensation also. All during the night the lamps threw their light on the exhibition bread on the Table. The unity of the whole nation is ever preserved before God, although its displayed unity was only of brief duration, and now a thing of the past. But God is ever true to His purpose. The nation as *one* is

ever before Him (see James i. 1). During these ages of
rejection—Israel, outcast of wearied breast and wandering
foot—the nation is preserved before God. If to man Israel is
a broken vessel, to God Israel yet lives, and shall in glory
yet to come, bask in the smile and under the immediate
government of her Messiah. Of all and more we have the
witness in the lamps shedding their light on the Table inside,
while outwardly all is dark and hopeless. In the light in
the sanctuary during the silence and darkness of the night,
we have a picture of the present, Israel downtrodden, the
nations in turmoil, and darkness brooding over the scene,
and the apostacy with its horrors soon to burst upon a
christless Christendom, but *above*, all is light, all is peace.
God sits upon the throne and all is well.

AARON AND THE LAMPS.

The children of Israel supplied the oil. We have our part
in that bright scene above. We instrumentally furnish the
material, but Aaron alone could light the lamps and keep them
burning. He lit the lamps in the evening which burned all
night till the morning, when he dressed them supplying
fresh oil and using the snuffers or tongs and snuff dishes.
This is what Christ is doing now. Our association with the
High Priest in heaven necessitates His priestly care,
intercession and sympathy. How many and varied are
His services. He first supplies the oil (Acts ii. 33); then
we bring it to Him, and He lights and trims the lamp, freely
using the snuffers so that the light may burn brightly.
There was no extinguisher provided. He may have to
remove all that hinders the light shining (Phil. ii. 15), but
extinguisher! there is none. The branch has to be purged

that it may bring forth *more* fruit. The light—so often dimmed and flickering—in us, may demand the free use of the tongs to remove the dead waste so that the light may shine brightly. But all is conducted in the sanctuary alone by our great High Priest; and His service of love never dies.

> " O light that followest all my way,
>   I yield my flickering torch to Thee ;
> My heart restores its borrowed ray,
> That in Thy sunshine's blaze its day
>   May brighter, fairer be."

The Table of Shewbread.

"Thou shalt also make a table of shittim wood : two cubits shall be the length thereof, and a cubit the breadth thereof, and a cubit and a half the height thereof.

"And thou shalt overlay it with pure gold, and make thereto a crown of gold round about.

"And thou shalt make unto it a border of an handbreadth round round, and thou shalt make a golden crown to the border thereof round about.

"And thou shalt make for it four rings of gold, and put the rings in the four corners that are in the four feet thereof.

"Over against the border shall the rings be for places of the staves to bear the table.

"And thou shalt make the staves of shittim wood, and overlay them with gold, that the table may be borne with them.

"And thou shalt make the dishes thereof, and spoons thereof, and covers thereof, and bowls thereof to cover withal: of pure gold shalt thou make them.

"And thou shalt set upon the table shewbread before Me alway" (Exod. xxv. 23-30).

THE TWELVE LOAVES.

"And thou shalt take fine flour, and bake twelve cakes thereof: two tenth deals shall be in one cake.

"And thou shalt set them in two rows, six on a row, upon the pure table before the LORD.

"And thou shalt put pure frankincense upon each row, that it may be on the bread for a memorial, even an offering made by fire unto the LORD.

"Every Sabbath he shall set it in order before the LORD continually, being taken from the children of Israel by an everlasting covenant.

"And it shall be Aaron's and his sons: and they shall eat it in the holy place: for it is most holy unto him of the offerings of the LORD made by fire by a perpetual statute" (Lev. xxiv. 5-9).

The principal Tabernacle-vessels were seven in number: (1) The Ark, (2) The Mercy-seat—these two spoke to the high priest in the most holy place; (3) The Altar of Incense, (4) The Candlestick, (5) The Table of Shewbread—those three spoke of Christ who leads our worship, and is also our light and food in the heavenly places; (6) The Brazen Altar of Sacrifice, (7) The Laver—those two stood in the Court; the former was for use by priests and people, the other was pre-eminently a priestly vessel.

In the most holy place—one vessel wholly of gold—the Mercy-seat. In the holy place—one vessel wholly of gold— the Candlestick. In the Court—one vessel wholly of brass—the Laver. *Gold* in the heavenly places, and *brass* for earth. The remaining vessels were made of two materials: shittim-wood and gold, or shittim-wood and brass. In the first temple there were *ten* tables, *ten* lavers, and *ten* candlesticks (2 Chron. iv.). This numeral expresses *responsibility to God*, and which in millennial times will be almost perfectly displayed. To that the temple looks forward.

The Table of Shewbread—the third of the sacred vessels in the holy place—was placed north, exactly opposite the Golden Candlestick (Exod. xl. 22, 24).* Shittim-wood and pure gold were the materials of which the Table was made. The basis was the shittim or acacia wood, the only timber used in the construction of the Tabernacle and its vessels. The measurements of the Table are carefully given: two cubits long, one cubit broad, and a cubit and a half in height (verse 23). The height is the same as the Ark (xxv. 10). In length and breadth the Ark exceeded the Table by a half cubit. Our communion at the Table never comes up to what the Ark and Mercy-seat are to God. What He rests on and finds there exceeds—far exceeds—our realizations. The dimensions of the Table will be better understood if we adopt English measurements. Thus, 36 inches in length, 18 inches in breadth, and 27 inches in

---

*In the closing chapter of Exodus we have it recorded seven times how faithfully all was done in exact accord with Jehovah's requirements: "*As the LORD commanded Moses*" (verses 19-29).

height.   The Table was overlaid with *pure* gold* : no
alloy could be allowed in that which set forth the Divine
nature of our Lord.   Thus, then, we have Christ in the
twofold glory of His Person—Divine and Human.   Christ
the Altars,† Christ the Laver, Christ the Candlestick, and
Christ the Table.   The Court and all in it uttered *that*
Name.   The holy place and its furniture, and the most holy
too, all spake of Jesus, God's beloved Son and our beloved
Lord.   But viewed as in heaven itself, His Person, His
Divine and human excellencies, His official and moral
glories, His offices, character, and sacrifice, form the burden
of the Tabernacle as a whole, down to the minutest
detail of pin and cord.   Christ is the story it unfolds.
Every whit of it uttereth His glory.

"Make thereto a crown of gold round about."   The word
"crown" in the text is nowhere used in the Scriptures to
denote the crown of royalty.   The meaning is that the
upper part of the Table had a gold moulding round about
of a highly ornamental character : see margin of R.V. of
Exod. xxv. 11, 24.

---

*The *gold* of the Ark, the Mercy-seat, the Table and its accessories, the
    Candlestick and its accessories, and the Altar of Incense must be
    pure.   Its absolute quality and purity are imperatively insisted upon.

†Blood was put upon the horns of both Altars : see Lev. iv. 7-18, as to the
    Golden Altar in the sanctuary, and verses 25, 30, 34 for the Brazen
    Altar in the Court.   This was done in the case of the ordinary sin-
    sacrifices.   But in the making of Atonement nothing is said as to the
    horns (Lev. i., xvi.).   Reader, either your sin is graven on the horns
    of the Altars (Jer. xvii. 1), or the blood is on those Altars—the witness
    that all has been blotted out for ever.

"The Brazen Altar smokes no more,
On which the victim lay."

"Thou shalt make unto it a border of an handbreadth round about, and thou shalt make a golden crown to the border thereof round about." The Table was finished by a border round of about four inches in width, while within the border, and resting on the Table, there was a crown of ornamental work. The border or cornice and its additional ornamental moulding, were meant to effectually secure the sanctified loaves, and all else on the Table, from slipping from their place. The handbreadth round about signified that a Divine hand safely guarded the loaves of communion. It was a Divine guarantee that on God's side there would be no failure in maintaining intact the food of the priests. Does not all this point to Christ on high, in Whose hands and by Whose hands we are ever sustained? The crown to the Table, and the crown to the border, point to Christ in His moral glory and excellency—not as on earth, but in God's own presence, as He is there (Heb. ii. 7).

> "In the heights of His bright glory,
>   Where the heavens rejoice,
> *I* have seen Him, *I* have known Him,
>   *I* have heard His voice."

Then four rings of gold were securely fastened to the feet of the Table—a ring to each of the four corners. The rings were placed just under the body of the Table, and were of sufficient strength and size to maintain the staves, which in their turn sustained the Table in its journeys. The *rings*, as presenting an unbroken circle, shadow forth the truth that Christ as a Divine Person (the *gold*), and also in the eternity of His Being (the *rings*), is the sustainer of His people, and as the gold rings and gold-covered staves indicated change and journey, so through all time and vicissitudes of life Christ shall surely uphold His own, supplying all needful food and refreshment by the way. God's provision for His people—at rest or in travel—is ample and divinely guaranteed. His resources are never diminished by the utmost demands of the pilgrim host. All the provisions of grace are maintained in the heavens, all our resources are there in Him. Christ is all and in all.

Then certain vessels, all of pure gold, were placed upon the Table. These vessels were kept in place and position by the handbreadth border, while *its* crown gave dignity to the Divine preservation of all—loaves and vessels—on the Table. The vessels are thus enumerated (xxxvii. 16): Dishes, spoons, bowls, covers or cups. The dishes were probably of more weight and value than the bowls, and are spoken of as "chargers" (Num. vii. 84)—a somewhat antiquated expression—a large hollow vessel probably employed to convey the loaves to and from the Table. The chargers or dishes of Num. vii. were of silver ; those for the sanctuary were of gold. The spoons were probably used for conveying the frankincense and putting it upon the "exhibition loaves" or "loaves of the presence," so termed from the significant fact that the bread was set before the Lord continually. In the account given in Exod. xxv. 29, we read of *cups* and bowls ; whereas in chap. xxxvii. 16 the reverse order is adopted—*bowls* and cups. We gather that "the strong wine" was first poured out of the large vessel—the bowl, into the smaller—the cup (Num. xxviii. 7). However that may be, it is evident that the bowls and cups—probably numbering twelve of each—were directly employed for the drink offerings unto Jehovah

—poured out in the holy place. We would also remark that " to cover withal," as in the descriptive account in Exodus, should read as in the margin, " to pour out." All these ministrations of priestly grace are carried on in the heavens ; they are heavenly in their sphere of action, but Divine in their operation. The holy place points to the former ; the gold vessels to the latter.

The Table in its wood and gold—our Lord in His Human and Divine natures—is in God's presence the support and and sustainer of our communion with Himself, and with the whole system of heavenly things. The Table sustained all placed upon it, and those things spoke of our communion. But our feeding upon Christ in the heavenlies is not unfolded here. *That* fittingly finds its place in Leviticus, hence the Exodus account of the Table of Shewbread closes with the brief statement : " And thou shalt set upon the table shewbread before me alway." The preparation of the loaves, their number, arrangement, and disposal, next claim our attention.

There were twelve loaves baked of fine flour only. No other ingredient was used—no leaven* (type of evil) nor honey (the mere sweetness of nature) : (Lev. ii. 11). The bruised corn, crushed and baken—exposed to the searching

---

*In all the varieties of the meat or flour offerings (Lev. ii.), honey and leaven were excluded, but oil (the Spirit) and salt (the preserving character of truth and grace) were essential ingredients. In Lev. xxiii. 15-21, we have detailed the feast of Pentecost which has its answer and fulfilment in Acts ii., two loaves of fine flour were to be baked *with leaven*. Those loaves, however, do not typify Christ, but present the Church in her actual state—sin in her. In Christ, we are unleavened, but as to our present and actual condition there is leaven (*evil*) in us.

action of fire—speaks of the absolute purity of His nature and life. The more thorough the fire, it the more manifested the purity of the fine flour. In us there is dross which trial makes manifest to ourselves, and, alas, to others. But in Christ, life's trials and even death itself, only manifested His absolute purity without and within. The purity of the flour was tested and its excellence proved in the baking process to which it was subjected. In Him, the fire manifested His life; in us, the fire separates the dross from the flour. In Christ the fire never separated. In Him the flour was pure. In us it is not so—it is a mixed quality. Each loaf was made of "two tenth deals" of flour; that is, each cake was made of two omers, or the fifth part of an ephah. One omer of manna was supplied from heaven daily for each of the Children of Israel—an ample amount for daily food (Exod. xvi.). But the cakes or loaves of Shewbread were each made just double that amount.* The numeral two expresses the fulness of Jewish and Gentile testimony—sufficient witness borne to the blessed truth that Christ known and loved on high, is the food of His heavenly people (John viii. 17; Rev. xi. 3, 4; Matt. xviii. 16). Type, fact, and experience unite in proclaiming the all-sufficiency of Christ in the heavenly sanctuary for the nourishment of each and all of the Lord's redeemed. "He is enough the mind and heart to fill."

Then the number and arrangement of the loaves have their own special teaching. The *twelve* loaves represented the *twelve* tribes of Israel. It is a singular circumstance that the only miracle common to the four Gospels is the feeding of the five thousand, the fragments of which filled

---

*About 10 lbs. weight.

twelve baskets (John vi. 9-13). It was Jesus in the power and grace of Jehovah feeding His people (Ps. cxxxii.). Israel, then, is represented in these twelve loaves on the Table. The unity of the nation to all outward appearance is gone for ever. Israel or the ten tribes is outcast and Judah dispersed (Isa. xi. 12). From the subversion of the ten-tribed kingdom by the Assyrian, and the subsequent destruction of the Judean monarchy by the Babylonian, there has been no re-union of the nation as such. The partial restoration of Judah and settlement in the land under Persian rule, was in no sense a restoration of the nation. In the year 70 A.D., the Roman ploughshare passed over Zion : the Temple laid in heaps, and the people dispersed throughout the earth. All seemed hopeless on the human side. But God is ever true to His word and promise. The future restoration, temporal blessing, and conversion of the whole nation of Israel are assured facts, and there are not wanting signs that the introduction of Israel into the scene of the world's troubled politics is nigh at hand (Ezek. xx.; xxxiv.; xxxvii. 15-28; Isa. lix. 20, 21). The cry of the prophet, "Ho, to the land "—the would-be deliverer of Judah from her dispersion of 2000 years—may be one translated into fact which many of us now alive will behold. The trend of events is distinctly Zionward. The Hebrew apostle James addresses his Epistle to " the twelve tribes which are scattered abroad." The nation as *one* ever exists before God. Israel is one people wrapped up in the thoughts and counsels of God, and her prophetic destiny is grandly assured. Israel is one, and the Church is one, spite of the world-wide scattering of both. Rule on earth— perfect government—will be expressed through Israel in a coming day : see Matt. xix. 28.

The cakes were set in two rows—six in each. In like manner the name of the Children of Israel were graven on two onyx stones—six on one stone, and six on the other. These stones were shoulder pieces borne by the high priest— stones of memorial (Exod. xxviii. 9-12). The twelve cakes too were for a memorial "before the LORD." Frank-incense—the moral beauties of Christ displayed in His life here below—was put upon the rows of bread—every cake had spread over it a precious covering of this delightful perfume. Thus Israel is ever before God in the moral perfectness of Christ, in all that He was and did as man on earth. Twelve* signifies *perfection of administration in Israel*—to be displayed in millennial times. How touching the thought that all during the long dark night of Israel's desolation—a broken vessel amongst the Gentiles—the sevenfold light of the sanctuary is thrown upon the twelve cakes on the pure Table covered with that which speaks of the beauty of Christ. Israel's present and future are dark to herself and to man. But both her unbelief, and the scorn and contempt of the   are alike to God. Israel is ever before Him, and witnessed in the sanctuary, she is a beauty to Jehovah.

The cakes remained in all their freshness on the Table for a week—a complete cycle of time. The fine flour set forth the perfectness of Christ, and covered with the frankincense the moral beauties of that wondrous life. There is then light and food in the heavenly places, and Christ is both. But the loaves were the food of the priests.

---

*This interesting numeral signifies *administrative perfection* on earth, for which see Rev. xxi. ; Deut. i. 23 ; Rev. xii. 1.

Every Sabbath freshly-baked cakes, fragrant with incense, were placed on the Table; the old ones removed and eaten by Aaron and his sons in *a* holy place—we presume the Court, which was such. Now, as we have repeatedly seen, Aaron's sons represent *all* believers in the Christian Dispensation—*all* are priests to God, and *all* have full and equal access into the heavenly sanctuary, and *all* have Christ in the blessed acceptability of His life and sacrifice to God, as their food. He is our light and our communion. *One* loaf to us; *twelve* to Israel. Israel's place and position was outside; it ever was and shall be. The place of the holy priesthood is inside; signified in type, and now made good in these Christian ages. It is Christians, Paul the profound worshipper, addresses in those words of priestly appeal, " Let us draw near " (Heb. x. 19-22).

This ordinance of the loaves comes under the designation of a " memorial," an " everlasting covenant," most holy of all the offerings," a " perpetual statute," while four times the " LORD " is expressly named in its connection. In drawing our remarks to a close, we would call attention to the fact that the Table of Shewbread is described immediately after the Ark. It is important to observe that while the Brazen Altar in the Court in its deep and profound teaching formed the basis of the whole Levitical system, yet the Ark in the Holiest was the centre of the Tabernacle within—it was the *first* manifestation or display of God to man; while the *last* point of approach from man to God. God begins with Christ, and we end with Him. He is the Alpha and the Omega, the first and the last.

But we must pass on from this truly delightful and fragrant theme, as other truths demand thought and meditation.

> Saviour of Thee we ne'er would tire :
>   The new and living food
> Can satisfy our heart's desire,
>   And life is in Thy blood.

The Beautiful Vail.

"And thou shalt make a vail of blue, and purple, and scarlet, and fine twined linen of cunning work: with cherubims shall it be made :

And thou shalt hang it upon four pillars of shittim wood overlaid with gold : their hooks shall be of gold upon the four sockets of silver " Exod. xxvi. 31, 32.

There may be differences of judgment in the interpretation of certain parts of the Tabernacle or vessels connected with it, but the spiritual signification of the Veil is placed beyond dispute. The Epistle to the Hebrews is a Divine commentary on the Levitical System as unfolded in the books of Exodus and Leviticus. In the tenth chapter of the epistle we read, "Having therefore, brethren, boldness to enter into the holiest by the blood of Jesus. By a new and living way which He hath consecrated for us through the Veil, *that is to say His flesh*" (verses 19, 20). But we must not confound *person* with *flesh*.

Christ viewed as a Person here on earth or as risen, and glorified, essentially differs from any created being. Angelic nature is one. Human nature is one. But the

Lord had a dual nature—Divine and Human; both in absolute harmony; both in absolute perfection. The Man Christ Jesus was none other than the Eternal Word become *flesh*. God manifest in *flesh*. Greater He could not be. But the *flesh* or humanity *He* assumed was not Himself. His "flesh" and "person" are by no means synonomous terms. The former refers to His holy humanity* (Luke i. 35), signified by the beautiful and separating Veil.

The Veil must have been an exquisite and beautiful example of the highest skill and design. The natural powers of the two chief artificers of the Tabernacle were under the immediate control of Jehovah—a Divine guarantee of the perfection and rare beauty of the work (Exod. xxxv. 30-35). There was neither gold nor wood in the Vail. *It was made in view of being rent.* Its basis was fine twined linen, but little of that could be seen as cherubic forms were wrought all over, and into the delicately prepared fabric in colours of blue, purple, and scarlet. The Veil was made Cherubim† (Exod. xxxvi. 35—delete "with" in the text); this the scenic representation of the executive, judicial power of God—the glory of the God of Israel which was driven from the Temple and City of Jerusalem (Ezek. x. 18, 19; xi. 22, 23) by the gross sin and idolatry of the people. Had it longer remained, righteousness must have swept Jerusalem and its guilty Temple, involving king,

---

*The sinlessness of the Lord's human nature is a feeble expression of the truth. His nature was holy and impeccable.

†The Cherubim do not represent the church or the redeemed. Genesis iii. 24 would forbid such an application. In the Mercy-seat which was all of gold pointing to what is wholly divine—the Cherubim were formed and fastened out of the *same* piece of gold—an integral part of the throne itself, hence cannot represent the Church.

priest, and people in one common judgment. But from the moment of the Incarnation the executive power of the throne of the Eternal was and is inseparably connected with that great fact. The government is upon His shoulders. The power of the throne occasionally broke out in the days of His flesh as when He trod upon the sea (Matt xiv. 25, 26), and calmed the raging elements of nature (Matt. viii. 26). His omnipotent power over Satan (Mark v. 1-15), over disease (verses 25-34), and over death (verses 35-43), proclaimed that the Cherubim had found their rest in Him.

In the future government of the world the power denoted by the Cherubim is witnessed in fullest exercise. He shall gloriously sway the sceptre in righteousness and execute His own decrees as Son of Man (John v. 27). Then the colours in which the Cherubim were wrought bear their testimony to Him as heavenly, in suffering, and in future glory; the Cherubim His government of the world.

The ten beautiful curtains which were thrown over the gold-covered boards were composed of the same material, colours and cherubic forms as the Veil—differing of course in dimensions. But in the description of the former, the basis (white linen) on which their beauties were displayed, is first mentioned (Exod. xxvi. 1); whereas in the account of the Veil the colours are first named (xxvi. 31). In the curtains* the purity of Christ is prominent—a purity fit for God and heaven. In the Veil the blue first attracts the sight directing us to Christ's association with heaven (John iii. 13).

---

*The hangings for the court were of same material. In the curtains it is Christ's purity in *heaven*, in the hangings, His purity as witnessed on *earth*.

The skilled work of the embroiderer is specially noted in the making of cherubic forms in the linen curtains, the Veil (Exod. xxvi), also the ephod and the breastplate of the High Priest (Chap. xxviii).

But how was the Veil suspended? It hung upon four pillars of shittim wood overlaid with gold. These pillars pointed to the Divine and Human, our Lord in the fulness of His Person—the God-Man. The pillars upheld the Veil. The pillars rested on silver sockets—massive blocks of silver each about a hundred and fourteen pounds weight and embedded in the ground.* The pillars were then immovable. The hooks above on which the Veil was suspended were of gold. The silver sockets sustained the pillars, while the gold sustained the Veil—gold above, silver beneath. The silver of *atonement* (Exod. xxx. 15-16) the basis, the gold of Divine Righteousness above. What a wondrous connection exists between those truths symbolised in the Veil, in the gold covered pillars, in the sockets of silver, and hooks of gold. The pillars were firmly planted on that glorious foundation—the blood of atonement.

"And thou shalt hang up the Veil under the taches that thou mayest bring thither within the Veil the ark of the testimony: and the Veil shall divide unto you between the holy place and the most holy" (verse 33). We have already remarked upon the relative dimensions of the two sacred apartments determined by the position of the Veil under

---

*We may remark that neither the sockets of brass, or silver were seen. There was that in the cross of which both sockets speak which man could not witness. " His *soul* was made an offering for sin " and *that* God alone could fathom.

the gold taches connecting the beautiful curtains.* The
smaller of the two, and but entered by the people's representative once a year was the holiest of all. The reader
would do well, however, to note the connection between the
beautiful curtains and the beautiful Veil as indicated in the
position of the latter under the taches of gold. Both the
curtains and the Veil speak of Christ. The former refer to
what He is abidingly in the Divine presence †; the latter
alone was rent in twain at His death. The Veil is the *flesh*
of Christ; the Veil rent is His *death*. The curtains were
never rent.

THE VEIL RENT.

The Veil of the Tabernacle and the Veil of the Temple
were identical: see Exod. xxxvi. for the former and
2 Chron. iii. 14 for the latter. Hebrews never speaks
of a rent Veil but supposes it. The rending of the Veil—
not its removal—is stated as an historical fact in each of the
synoptical gospels. Its symbolic force and value is of the
last importance to all.

The fact that the rending of the Temple Veil is noted
three times as one of the greatest circumstances consequent
upon the death of our Lord, marks it as profoundly significant. Several questions naturally suggest themselves to
thoughtful readers: why was the Veil rent? why rent from
top to bottom? (Matt. and Mark). Why rent in the midst?
(Luke).

---

*See page 65.
†" Jesus Christ the righteous " One (1 John ii. 1).

Why was the Veil rent? Historically it was the Veil of the *Temple* that was rent, but in the Epistle to the Hebrews the apostle never once refers to the Temple. He reverts in his precious lessons and truths to the primary and fundamental idea—the Tabernacle—especially Chaps. ix; x. He speaks of the Veil of the *Tabernacle*. The Evangelists of the Veil of the *Temple*. The Veil was the link of connection between the two (x. 19-20). Now the Incarnation and the Death of the Lord, or the Manger and the Cross, each have their respective thoughts and teaching. In the former it is *God coming out to man* revealing Himself to His creatures : in the latter it is *God opening the door—a righteous and holy One—for men to enter His presence.*

Hence it was needful for the Veil to be torn asunder if a creature sinful in himself, could righteously enter the Divine presence. It intimated the death of the Lord of the Temple, and consequently the complete setting aside of the whole Jewish system of sacrifice and worship. If the Veil is rent, if that which divided the holy from the most holy, and hid the glory and presence of God from all, is rent, then with unsandalled feet and in boldness of soul with the blood of Jesus as our only plea we draw near. Our place as worshippers is in the immediate presence of God—for us there is no Veil. The holy place and the holiest are one. For 500 years the beautiful Veil hung in silent glory, confining and concealing the glory and presence of Jehovah to one small apartment, and effectually shutting out all save Aaron, who only once a year could enter the sacred presence and that not without incense and blood. The glories of the Tabernacle were centred in Jesus. The Tabernacle so to speak was in Him. His *flesh* is the Veil. But the fact of

Incarnation blessed as it is could not set one in God's presence. Jesus died. The Veil was rent and thus and then the open door to God's immediate presence. Christ on earth was the beautiful Veil. "The word became flesh and tabernacled among us and we behold His glory "(John i. 14). The faith of some pierced through the outer covering, the rough exterior of the badgers skins, and beheld and feasted upon the hidden glories within. But the perfect and holy humanity of our Lord was brought to the Altar. He died. The Veil was rent. Behold heaven is now *open*.

No Israelite of old could approach beyond the Brazen Altar—not even to the Laver which was a priestly vessel. Not even the most favoured of Levites dare look into the Tabernacle under pain of death (Num. iv. 19-20). The priests of old in their daily ministration in the sanctuary, without doubt looked upon the Veil and wondered and worshipped, but none save the anointed High Priest could enter the holiest of all, and when He did so, all were banished from the Tabernacle on that most sacred of occasions. Unhallowed approach has but one penalty—*death*. Why all this distance and dread ? Simply because sin could not be permitted in God's holy, holy, holy presence ; nor could a sin burdened conscience be at peace or rest there. Who could look upon the uncreated and glorious Majesty of God and live ?

The repetition of sacrifice could not perfect the worshippers, nor effectually remove sin from the conscience, on the contrary the *remembrance*, of sins, not the *blotting* of them out was proclaimed aloud by every fresh sacrifice (Heb. x. 1-4). The fire of judgment was ever demanding sacrifice, and was never satisfied. Now we know of a sacrifice infinite in its worth and value—one which has consumed the fire of Divine wrath, and it burns no more. "For by one offering He hath PERFECTED FOR EVER them that are sanctified" (Heb. x. 14). Now the Sacrifice of Christ—of Himself—has accomplished three things—incapable of repetition. *First*, it has answered to the full the claims of the Throne of Jehovah. *Second*, it has perfected the conscience of the believer for ever. *Third*, it has righteously opened a way—new and living— into the very presence of God Himself.

Why rent from *top* to *bottom?* It must have been effected by a Divine hand and for a Divine purpose. Thus through this symbolic act a blood-stained way is now open from God to man, from heaven to earth. It was God's own hand that rent the Veil. It was God's own hand that smote the Rock of Ages that the gushing streams might flow out and forth (Zech. xiii. 7).

Why rent in the *midst?* Because there is now an open and straight door into God's presence. It is not a circuitous way. There is no *side* entrance; one open door to all. No one can, save wilfully, mistake the way to God. The door of the Tabernacle and the Veil faced each other, in an exact line with the Brazen Altar—the first point of contact with God. The start—the Altar in the Court; the goal—the Ark in the Holiest.

The Veil is termed in Heb. ix. 3 "the *second* Veil;" the first being the door into the Tabernacle. The first Veil was suspended on *five* pillars*; the second Veil on four pillars*. There are *five* inspired writers who severally and

---

*The pillars of the Court were ornamented at the top—silver fillets. But neither the five nor four pillars of the Tabernacle had ornamental capitals.

together introduce us to Christ on high. There are *four* Gospels in which the Veil—the absolute humanity of our Lord in peerless perfection and purity is depicted.

It is also termed "the covering Veil" (Num. iv. 5; Exod. xxxix. 34), as it was used to cover the Ark when journeying, and effectually screened it from view when the Tabernacle was at rest (Exod. xl. 3). What does all this signify? The presence of God could not be entered, His glory within could not be witnessed so long as the Veil stood unrent and the Mercy-seat unstained by blood—the witness of death. The Veil is rent, now all is changed and all rests on the magnificent and solitary foundation THE DEATH OF OUR LORD JESUS CHRIST FOR OUR SINS.

The Ark of the Covenant.

"AND they shall make an Ark of shittim wood: two cubits and a half shall be the length thereof, and a cubit and a half the breadth thereof, and a cubit and a half the height thereof.

"And thou shalt overlay it with pure gold, within and without shalt thou overlay it, and shalt make upon it a crown of gold round about.

"And thou shalt cast four rings of gold for it, and put them in the four corners thereof; and two rings shall be in the one side of it, and two rings in the other side of it.

"And thou shalt make staves of shittim wood, and overlay them with gold.

"And thou shalt put the staves into the rings by the sides of the Ark, that the Ark may be borne with them.

"The staves shall be in the rings of the Ark: they shall not be taken from it.

" And thou shalt put into the Ark the testimony which I shall give thee " (Exod. xxv. 10-16).

We now enter the most sacred spot on earth. The Holiest was a square apartment of 15 feet in breadth, length, and height,—a figure of the Heaven of heavens. The Holy of holies must be entered with bowed head and unsandalled feet for Jehovah on His throne is there. How awful the presence chamber of the LORD of Hosts. Here no human voice is heard, only the voice of God. Here no seat for man is found, Jehovah alone sits and that on the throne of glory and righteousness. Here no created light, as sun, nor artificial light, as the candle, illumines the apartment, the glory of God fills the Holiest with its own Divine radiance. Here too all is Divine and we breathe another atmosphere than that of this creation. There were but two men in all Israel permitted to enter the Holiest ; these were Aaron, Israel's first and greatest high priest, and Moses, Israel's only mediator—both typical of Christ.

We enter into the *immediate* presence of God through the rent Veil—the *death* of Christ, yet strange to say, it is a *new* and *living* way (Heb. x. 20). The sacrifice accepted by God is the alone ground of entrance into the presence and home of *the* Eternal. The Ritualism of Israel was a combination of shadows of which CHRIST is the glorious substance. The Ritualism of Christendom is an empty farce. Christianity in its *realities* stands out in sharp contrast to Christendom with its worse than meaningless ritualistic shadows. In Christ risen and glorified we see the force and substance of Ritualism at its best, as witnessed in its birthplace and native home—Judaism of old whether in Tabernacle or Temple.

Exactly facing the beautiful Veil with its wondrous story of Christ, stood the Ark—the most unique of all the holy vessels. Its lid or covering was the pure gold Mercy-seat or propitiatory (Rom. iii. 25). Either word means to *cover*, hence the Mercy-seat exactly covered the Ark in length and breadth—neither more nor less. The Ark is the Person of Christ. The sacrifice is the ground, and the blood sprinkled Mercy-seat the place, where God can meet any one coming to Him in faith. But the Atonement itself carries with it the full value of the One who made it. The sacrifice is of infinite worth, for this is measured by the Person of our Lord. Christ and the Sacrifice are of equal value for He in His dual Person—Divine and Human—was the Sacrifice. This we believe is the profound lesson in the precise adjustment of the Mercy-seat to the Ark.

The Ark and the Mercy-seat combined formed the throne of God in Israel, but they may be separately treated, as indeed they are in the Mosaic description. Christ as the Ark forms a complete type of Divine truth by itself. There was no necessity in His nature why He should become a propitiatory for our sins, save in obedience to the will of God (Heb. x. 9), and the necessity of love. He voluntarily gave Himself up to accomplish our redemption (John x. 15, 17, 18).

The Ark was made of shittim-wood and gold. Its measurements are carefully prescribed by the Divine command; no alteration or attempted improvement could be allowed. The various things made, must be according in all respects to the heavenly pattern shown to Moses on the mount; not the slightest deviation would be permitted. If man had been left to his own ingenuity or skill to construct a dwelling place for Jehovah on earth, then we never could have had those foreshadows of Christ, for "no man knoweth the Son but the Father" (Matt. xi. 27). The whole Mosaic ritual is an elaborate foreshadowing of Christ in His Person, Offices, and Services. No creature mind could have conceived such a character either as a whole or in part as typified in the Levitical system.

We may have some difficulty in assigning a reason for each of the measurements of the Ark, but the reader may rest assured that God meant certain lessons in these carefully prescribed numbers of cubits, and our inability to lay hold fully of these teachings should the more cast us in humble dependence upon the grace and help of the Holy Spirit— the sole Interpreter of the written Word.

Then the shittim-wood—said not to rot, and hence termed *incorruptible*—was entirely covered over with pure gold within and without, and then ornamented with a crown of gold round about. The dual Person of our Lord as the God-man and the moral glory of His Person (John i. 14) are thus indicated. The Ark was a chest in which were deposited the unbroken tables of the law received by the lawgiver on his second ascent to the mount. The law in all its holy and righteous requirements was broken by the people. But the law lay unbroken in the heart of Jesus, "Yea, Thy law is within my heart" (Ps. xl. 8). Thus the unbroken tables of the law in the centre of the Ark were clearly typical of the law of God in the heart of the Lord.

Subsequently there were deposited in the sacred chest, a golden pot of manna*—the bread from heaven with which

---

*Termed "angels' food" (Ps. lxxviii. 25), and "the bread of God" (John vi. 33). The manna figures Christ in *humiliation* (John vi. 31-51). "The old corn of the land" (Joshua v. 10-12) Christ in *glory*.

God miraculously fed His people in the wilderness (Exod. xvi. 32-36)—a perpetual reminder of Jehovah's faithfulness in the desert. It is to this hidden manna that Rev. ii. 17 refers. In the side of the Ark the Pentateuch written by Moses, was carefully deposited by the Levites, and jealously guarded by the whole nation (Deut. xxxi. 24-26). Its very existence seems to have been forgotten till accidently discovered by Hilkiah the priest 800 years afterwards (2 Chron. xxxiv. 14-22). The Ark also contained Aaron's rod that budded (Num. xvii.). In the holiest, but not deposited in the Ark, stood the golden censer (Heb. ix. 4) used but once a year—on the day of Atonement (Lev. xvi.).

The Ark is the first named of Sanctuary Vessels, and the first made ready to receive the testimony given by Jehovah to the lawgiver.

When the Ark was transferred from the Tabernacle to the Temple, there was nothing in it save the two tables of stone (1 Kings viii. 9). The law was the measure of God's righteous claim upon man and this demand cannot be dispensed with. However richly grace reigns, righteousness must be maintained, hence the moral foundation on which Israel stood before Jehovah, whether in the wilderness or in the land, whether under grace or glory, was RIGHTEOUSNESS. The Ark was the expression of Divine *righteousness*, the Mercy-seat sets forth Divine *grace*. In length and breadth the Ark and Mercy-seat were the same. The two exactly fitted each other and together constituted the Throne of Jehovah in the midst of Israel—the Ark His Throne, the Tabernacle His Dwelling-place. Not only did the Mercy-seat exactly cover the golden chest, but where they met must have been hidden from view by the golden crown encircling it. It thus formed one complete whole, a grand combination of righteousness and grace in the Person of our Adorable Lord, now crowned with glory and honour. Judgment upon sinful and transgressing Israel *must* have been the certain result had the Ark not been covered. The blood-sprinkled Mercy-seat covering the Ark guarded by the ministers of God's executive government—the Cherubim—maintained and upheld the righteous character of God in justifying and receiving to Himself the vilest of the vile.

The vessels of the Tabernacle were inferior in size and number to those of the Temple, while the Ark was the only vessel common to both buildings. The second and third Temples had no Ark, and we are certain from Jer. iii. 16 that the millennial Temple will not have one, nor will it ever be thought of by redeemed and happy Israel, for that which the Ark of God typified—the presence of Jehovah with His people—will be an accomplished fact. We have no record of the Ark being removed from Solomon's Temple by the Babylonian Conqueror of Judah. Tradition asserts that Jeremiah who was in Jerusalem during the prolonged siege, or one of the priests concealed it. The fate of the Ark is a matter of the merest conjecture and profitless speculation.

The following are the terms used of the Ark :—

The Ark of the Testimony (Exod. xxv. 22).
The Ark of the Covenant (Num. x. 33).
The Ark of the Lord God (1 Kings ii. 26).
The Ark of the LORD (Joshua iii. 13).
The Ark of God (1 Sam. iii. 3).

The Holy Ark (2 Chron. xxxv. 3).

The Ark of Thy Strength (Ps. cxxxii. 8).

Termed also "His Strength" and "His Glory" (Ps. lxxviii. 61).

The rings and staves—four of the former, two of the latter—intimate that Jehovah took His part in the journeyings of His people. Were they on travel?—Jehovah would accompany them every foot of the way. The staves of shittim-wood and gold—Christ with His people till the end of the age (Matt. xxviii. 20), is a precious truth. The staves "*shall not be taken from it*" (Exod. xxv. 15), intimate the adaptability of Christ and His instant readiness to travel with His own, whether in land or sea, valley or mountain—Christ is with us. But when travelling days were over, when the wilderness had given place to the land, and glory and rest were reached through the infinite grace of Jehovah, the Ark was transferred to the Temple; the staves which told of pilgrim travel were withdrawn (1 Kings viii. 8)—seen *inside*, never again outside. In heaven the remembrance of Christ with us in the journeys and experiences of the wilderness, will be one of the richest joys of the paradise of God.

The Ark with its golden crown round about, foreshadowed the Person of our Lord glorified on high, its rings and staves Christ's travels with His people. We may here remark that the Tabernacle, as its name implied, was intended for wilderness travel and need. The Temple was an elaboration of the Tabernacle, and in its very nature expressed a settled condition in the land.

THE HISTORY OF THE ARK.

The Ark was the only sacred vessel which could be viewed apart from its place in the Tabernacle, and, in point of fact, its strange and eventful history lies outside its proper and nominal place in the midst of the many thousands of Israel, as their centre. It was the *priests* who covered the holy vessels preparatory to the journeys of the camp. It was the *Levites* who carried on their shoulders the Ark and other holy vessels. But on three occasions it was borne on the shoulders of priests. When the camp was at rest the Ark was the centre; with the Mercy-seat it constituted Jehovah's throne. From thence Israel was governed, instructed, and cared for.

Two silver trumpets were made. These were to be blown by the priests—first, for the calling of the assembly; second, for the journeying of the camps (Num. x. 2, 8). But, first, Aaron and his sons enter the Holiest, take down the beautiful Veil separating the two holy apartments, and with it cover the Ark; then the Veil was covered over completely with badgers' skins, and over all a cloth wholly of blue (Num. iv. 5, 6). Then the sons of Kohath had committed to them the happy service of carrying the holy vessels from place to place. But Jehovah so jealously guarded all that expressed Himself to men that death was the penalty for any save the priests who touched any holy thing or looked within (verses 15, 20). This accounts for the judgment executed upon Uzzah who dared to put his hand upon the Ark to steady it (2 Sam. vi. 7). God ever sees to it that His glory is maintained. It needs not the rude hand of man to maintain the Ark of our God. The Ark is never in peril.

THE ORDER OF THE MARCH.

The order in which Israel in her tribes was to journey
is carefully marked out in Numbers x. Six tribes marched
in front, and six in the rear. Between these, and thus in
the very centre of the camp, the Ark was borne on the
shoulders of the Kohathites. But behind the first three
tribes the Tabernacle was borne (verse 17). Thus in the
march the Tabernacle preceded, so that it could be
set up to receive the Ark (verse 21). The order under
Moses is the same under Asaph (Ps. lxxx. 1, 2). When the
Ark set forward (for *it*, not the camp nor even the Tabernacle, was the subject of surpassing interest), Moses uttered
the calm, yet triumphant appeal to Jehovah, "Rise up,
LORD, and let Thine enemies be scattered, and let them
that hate Thee flee before Thee," and Jehovah again and
again in the subsequent history of the Ark answered the
appeal of the mediator (Num. x. 35). The same cry will
be taken up by the future suffering remnant of Israel
(Ps. lxviii. 1)—only, in their case, their thoughts will be
directed to God *Himself*, the Ark being no longer in
existence. When the Ark rested, Moses said, "Return,
O Lord, unto the many thousands of Israel." The presence
of Jehovah there was signified by the Ark.

But while Jehovah carefully instructed His people as to
the order of the march—the Ark in the centre—yet in this
very chapter (Num. x.), where the movements of the camp
are Divinely ordered, there is a distinct departure from that
order. Why this? Hobab, father-in-law to Moses, who
had an intimate knowledge of the wilderness, was earnestly
requested by the law-giver to act as guide to the journeying
host: "thou mayest be to us instead of eyes" (verse 31).

Hobab as guide instead of Jehovah! The eyes of a man instead of the eyes of God! Jehovah resents the suggestion of His servant; even Hobab seemed to have a deeper sense of God's presence with and for His people than Moses. "The ark of the covenant of the LORD went BEFORE them in the three days' journey to search out a resting place for them" (verse 33). Thus the order of the march was reversed. The Ark went *before* the camp, not as in the prescribed order in the centre. Laws are made for the creature, but the Creator knows no law, is not controlled by law, save by the law of His own nature. Law, dispensation, and economic arrangements must all yield to the claim of need. God ever answers the necessities of the creature as such, whatever law or laws may stand in the way. These may have to be brushed aside so that the law of Divine love may be honoured.

There was another instance of departure from the order of march, as prescribed in Numbers x. We refer to the crossing of the Jordan (Joshua iii. 3, 4). But it is well to notice that the order of march, as detailed by Moses (Num. x.), was for the journeyings of the wilderness. The people settled in the land, but travelled in the wilderness.

THE EVENTFUL HISTORY OF THE ARK IN THE LAND.

We necessarily start with the passage of the Jordan. The trumpet and the cloud characterised the departure of the redeemed host on their wilderness journey. But the entrance into Canaan was effected in the value of the Ark alone. Israel crossed the Red Sea under the protection of the cloud, and crossed the Jordan under the shelter of the Ark. In both cases the cloud and the Ark in

themselves were of no avail, it was what they respectively
signified that was of account.   When the camp was at rest,
the position of the Ark in the Holiest was indicated by the
pillar of cloud which rested over the Shekinah, or glory
cloud inside.   Here, however, (Joshua iii.) we have no
cloud; the Ark alone is named.   The Ark was borne on
the shoulders of the priests, and preceded the host by about
a mile distance.   The moment the priests entered the overflowing river, the waters above and beneath for about 20
miles were rolled back, and the host passed over.   Christ
entered the river of death for us.   What was death to Him,
is firm and dry ground to us.   The Red Sea was Christ
in death for us.   The Jordan signified our death with
Him.   Christ's death (the Red Sea) secures our Redemption.   Our death with Him (the Jordan) is our
door of entrance into the heavenly places.   The typical
import of the "Sea" and the "River" is of profound
interest to every believer.   In brief it may be thus
stated.   The Red Sea signifies Christ's death for us so that
the glory and strength of *God's Salvation* may be ours.
The close of Rom. iv. and opening of chap. v. may illustrate
this.   The crossing of the Jordan then overflowing all its
banks, points to our association with Him in death—only
He first—in order that a dry and safe passage and secure
anchorage ground may be ours : see John xiii. 33-36 ; Eph.
ii. 1-6.   We may further remark that type and symbol
necessarily fall short in presenting the truth in its fulness.
In this instance the sea and the river—geographically and
historically separated—coalesce in the typical instruction
It is the one death of Christ, but viewed in different
aspects.

Now Jericho, the centre and seat of the enemy's strength, must fall before the conquering host. Tidings had reached the whole country of Jehovah's acts of power on behalf of His people, and a general fear and terror had taken possession of all—kings, princes, and people (Joshua ii. 9, 11, 24). The world *to-day* is uneasy. It knows in its heart that God is with and for His people, however much the feeling may be disguised and concealed from public view (Phil. i. 28). The very presence of danger emboldens the child of God, strengthens faith, and inspires patient waiting to see how God will signalise His own Name. Thus in the maintenance of the glory of God our safety is amply secured.

The saved host encompass the city, but no human weapon is directed against those impregnable walls. On this occasion the Ark was in the centre, borne on the shoulders of the priests, not the Kohathites. This was the second instance of the Kohathites being displaced by the priests bearing the Ark. In the passage of the Jordan the Ark went first; in the downfall of Jericho the Ark was in the centre of the host. The armed men preceded the Ark, priests, and trumpeters, while the people followed in the rear. The order of march as appointed in Numbers x. was not exactly that adopted in Joshua vi., but it has to be remembered that the Mosaic instructions concerned the *wilderness*, while those issued by Joshua applied to the *land*.

The measures adopted for the overthrow of the city were in themselves insignificant and humbling to human pride. The respite granted—seven days—must have been a time of anxiety to besiegers and besieged. But the end was sure. The lofty walls and strong towers must fall before the Ark of Jehovah. To human observation it was weakness against strength. The Ark symbolised the presence of the LORD of Hosts, and before it the utmost strength of the enemy was powerless. "Shout, for the LORD hath given you the city." The LORD triumphed over *death*, the Jordan, and over *Satan*, Jericho. The person or people who have the conscious assurance of God's presence, are for the time being omnipotent. "Confide ye in Jehovah for ever ; for in Jah, Jehovah is the Rock of Ages" (Isa. xxvi. 4).

We next read of the Ark in that interesting scene recorded in Deut. xi. 26-32 and Josh. viii. 30-35—only in the Mosaic account the Ark is not mentioned. The conquest of Canaan was not yet complete, but the Jordan crossed, and Jericho and Ai destroyed, abundantly confirmed the prophetic word that the whole land from north to south and from west to east was granted to Israel by a Divine charter (Gen. xiii. 14-17; xv. 18-21; xvii. 8). But while without fail the land in its entirety shall yet be possessed by the Jewish people—for these Abrahamic promises were unconditional and pledged for by the word and oath of Jehovah—yet the possession of Palestine under Joshua was conditional on the people's obedience and faithfulness, and in these they miserably came short. The scene, however, in the valley lying between Mounts Ebal and Gerizim is one of deepest interest. All Israel are gathered together—princes, priests, women, children, and strangers. Half of the tribes are on the one mount, and the other six on the opposite mount—the Ark between borne thither on the shoulders of the priests—the third occasion of their doing so. The formal possession of the land—the gift of Jehovah to His people—was the occasion of the unusual proceedings on that hallowed ground. The Ark was the centre of all, for it was Jehovah who really took possession, but He did so in His people.

THE ARK—JEHOVAH'S STRENGTH AND GLORY—IN CAPTIVITY.

The next occasion in which the Ark is prominently brought before us is recorded in 1 Sam. iv. If in Joshua we have narrated the *victories* of Israel, we have in Judges their *failures* equally written down, for our instruction surely—on whom the ends of the ages have come (1 Cor. x. 11). The last five chapters of the book of Judges present a dark and lurid picture. Now, our chapter (1 Sam. iv.) opens with a battle fought between Israel and the Philistines, in which the former were defeated, with the loss of four thousand men. There was no enquiry at the Lord *why* they were defeated, no mourning before Him, no supplications addressed to the LORD of Hosts, no tears of repentance and sorrow shed before Him. The Ark was sent for out of Shiloh, where it rested in its rightful place in the Tabernacle and between the Cherubim. "Let us fetch the Ark of the Covenant of the LORD out of Shiloh unto us, that when *it* cometh among us *it* may save us out of the hand of our enemies." It was not *that* made by Bezaleel that ever did or could save. Jehovah was the Saviour of His people. The typical force and value of the Ark consisted in that magnificent truth for Israel as for us: God amongst His people and for them. The Ark in itself could no more deliver Israel than could the gods of the heathen deliver Philistia. "When *it* cometh among us." What was the value of the Ark unless it pointed to God and His presence?—that "*it* may save us." Had it ever done so? Was it the mere Ark of shittim and gold that arrested the rushing, overflowing waters of Jordan? that caused the mighty walls of Jericho to crumble to pieces? Nay, it was Jehovah. Not *it* but *He* delivered and shall deliver.

When faith in the living God is given up, then ordinances supplant Him in the mind and heart.

Israel was smitten with a great slaughter, thirty thousand at least fell on that fatal battlefield, including the sons of Eli, and worse still the Ark of God was taken. It is to this that the psalmist refers, "He delivered His strength into captivity, and His glory into the enemy's hand" (lxxviii. 61). The Ark, the glory and strength, not of Israel but of Jehovah, is in the hands of the uncircumcised and triumphing heathen.

The Ark is taken, the glory is departed from Israel (1 Sam. iv. 21, 22). The Ark was brought to Ashdod, and deposited in triumph in the temple of Dagon. During the night, unseen by all, Jehovah awoke for His glory. Early in the morning when the Ashdodites visited the house of their deity, they found Dagon lying on his face on the ground before the Ark of the LORD. Perhaps it was an accident, so Dagon was put upon his feet again, but the following morning witnessed a scene unequalled in the history of the Philistines. "Dagon was fallen upon his face to the ground before the Ark of the LORD: and the head of Dagon and both the palms of his hands were cut off upon the threshold; only the stump of Dagon was left to him" (1 Sam. v. 4.). God amply justified His name and glory for during the seven months the Ark was in the country of the Philistines (chaps. v; vi. 1 Sam.) it was a period of sharp judgment. The most awful was that which befel the men of Beth-shemesh of Israel, who impiously looked into the Ark. To do so they must have removed the covering—the Mercy-seat of pure gold on which the blood of atonement had been sprinkled. The law can only condemn; it is the blood that saves. The law in the Ark without its blood-sprinkled cover must have been judgment—pure and simple. It was an awful slaughter 50,070 men! Wherever the Ark went in Philistia, judgment to people and land tracked its steps. That which was the highest blessing to Israel proved the deepest curse to the Philistines. The former were a redeemed people, hence the Ark was in their midst for blessing; the latter were a heathen nation, and thus the Ark could only be amongst them for judgment.

Then the Ark was removed to Kirjath-jearim, where it remained twenty years (1 Sam. vii. 1, 2). On the accession of David to the throne, both king and people remembered the Ark. The joy could not be complete without the visible presence of God amongst them. Amidst a scene of rejoicing the Ark was put on a new cart. It should have been borne on the shoulders of priests or Levites. One wrong step led to another. Uzzah put forth his hand to steady it. "And the anger of the LORD was kindled against Uzzah: and God smote him there for his error: and there he died by the Ark of God" (2 Sam. vi.). Thus did God vindicate His word (Numb. iv. 15). It was death for any save priests to touch the holy vessels, or even to look into them when uncovered.

The progress of the Ark to Jerusalem was thus arrested. It was carried aside into the house of Obed-edom, where it remained for three months. It was a brief but blessed season to Obed-edom and all his household.

The next stage in the journey of the Ark was from the house of Obed-edom to the City of David, but on this occasion the order prescribed by Jehovah was strictly

adhered to, being carried by its staves on the shoulders of
the Kohathites. David had learnt the lesson that "*every
transgression and disobedience received a just recompense
of reward*" (Heb. ii. 2). The men of Beth-shemesh, and Uzzah
were striking examples of this. Music, dancing, singing,
sacrifice, and a scene of rejoicing unequalled previously in
the history of Israel, marked the progress of the Ark to its
final resting place (2 Sam. vi. 12-19; 1 Chron. xv.). The
gladsome day was not overcast by any act of judgment as
on the former stage of the journey. The Ark never again
entered the Tabernacle, but was placed in a new tent or
tabernacle which David had prepared for its special use
(2 Sam. vi. 17).

Finally, David urged on the preparations for the building
of the Temple, so that the Ark and other holy vessels might
be deposited in a house, and amidst surroundings worthy of
such sacred and precious vessels (1 Chron. xxii. 19).

Solomon, who succeeded his father on the throne of the
LORD, had the high honour of conveying the Ark from
David's tent to its rightful place in the Temple. It was
carried by the priests and placed between the Cherubim,
the staves were then drawn out as its journeys were over
(1 Kings viii. 6-11; 2 Chron. v.). Thus the *only* Tabernacle
Vessel was installed in the Oracle or Adytum of the Temple
where it remained till the Chaldean destruction of Jerusalem. What ultimately became of it, we know not.
Its fate is shrouded in mystery. *We* have that which the
Ark set forth—the Divine presence. A material Ark now
would be useless. For Christians, ritualism, holy places,
and shadows are past—CHRIST IS ALL.

"WORTHY THE LAMB."

" 'Tis the Church triumphant singing, 'Worthy the Lamb ;'
Heaven throughout with praises ringing, ' Worthy the Lamb.'
  Thrones and powers before Him bending,
  Odours sweet and voice ascending,
  Swell the chorus, never ending—' Worthy the Lamb !'

Every kindred, tongue, and nation, ' Worthy the Lamb ;'
Join to sing the great salvation, ' Worthy the Lamb.'
  Loud as mighty thunders roaring,
  Floods of mighty waters pouring,
  Prostrate at His Feet adoring—' Worthy the Lamb !'

Harps and songs for ever sounding, ' Worthy the Lamb ;'
Mighty grace o'er sin abounding, ' Worthy the Lamb.'
  By His blood He dearly bought us,
  Wand'ring from the fold He sought us,
  And to glory safely brought us—' Worthy the Lamb !'

Sing with blest anticipation, ' Worthy the Lamb ;'
Through the vale of tribulation, ' Worthy the Lamb.'
  Sweetest notes, all notes excelling,
  On the theme for ever dwelling,
  Still untold, though ever telling—' Worthy the Lamb !' "

The Mercy-seat.

"And thou shalt make a Mercy-seat of pure gold: two cubits and a half shall be the length thereof, and a cubit and a half the breadth thereof.

And thou shalt make two Cherubims of gold, of beaten work shalt thou make them, in the two ends of the Mercy-seat.

And make one Cherub on the one end, and the other Cherub on the other end : even of the Mercy-seat shall ye make the Cherubims on the two ends thereof.

And the Cherubims shall stretch forth their wings on high, covering the Mercy-seat with their wings, and their faces shall look one to another; toward the Mercy-seat shall the faces of the Cherubim be.

And thou shalt put the Mercy-seat above upon the Ark; and in the Ark thou shalt put the testimony that I shall give thee.

And there I will meet with thee, and I will commune with thee from above the Mercy-seat, from between the two Cherubims which are upon the Ark of the testimony, of all things which I will give thee in commandment unto the children of Israel" (Exod. xxv. 17-22).

In the construction of the Mercy-seat there was no wood, nor any other metal save gold, and that of the purest. It points to what is intrinsically Divine. The Ark of wood and gold directs to the Person of the Lord in Whom the Divine and Human natures are united, yet but *one* Person. Thus the *Word* (the gold) became *flesh* (the wood): see John i. 14: 1 Tim. iii. 16. "God manifest in flesh." The Mercy-seat views Christ as a Divine Person apart from incarnation.

The size of the Mercy-seat in length and breadth was precisely that of the Ark. The adjustment was perfect. The top of the Ark was surmounted with a rim of gold as a border round about, hence when the Mercy-seat was set above upon the Ark (verse 21), the crown or rim of gold round about would conceal from view where the two were joined. One complete picture of Christ is thus presented, yet the Mercy-seat may be separately regarded (1 Chron. xxviii. 11).

The Mercy-seat or propitiatory is the typical representation of Christ, " Whom God hath set forth a *propitiation* through faith in His blood, to declare His (God's) righteousness for the remission of sins that are past, through the forbearance of God : to declare at this time His righteousness : that He might be just and the Justifier of him which believeth in Jesus " (Rom. iii. 25-26). The Mercy-seat or propitiatory could only be such when sprinkled with the blood of atonement. The blood on the gold righteously enabled God in the absolute consistency of His Being to sit on the Mercy-seat and dispense mercy to those who approach Him : nay, even higher still, it became a throne of relationship and communion. " And there I will meet with thee, and I will commune with thee from above the Mercy-seat, from between the two cherubim which are upon the Ark of the testimony, of all things which I will give thee in commandment unto the children of Israel " (verse 22).

The Ark was God's throne ; the basis of it was the Mercy-seat, whilst its supporters were the two " Cherubim of glory " (Heb. ix. 5). Thus the typical representation of God's throne was set up in the Holiest—figure of the Heaven of heavens. The Ark and all pertaining to it point *up* to the throne of Jehovah " the throne of the Majesty in the heavens " (Heb. viii. 1). It is a throne of holiness, of righteousness, of grace, and, of course, as the very term denotes, one of government. From it the universe is governed. It is the first sight in the heavenly scene beheld by the Seer of Patmos (Rev. iv. 2).

Thus the Ark and its pure gold lid—the Mercy-seat—was the throne of *government* over all beings; the throne of *relationship* to Israel; and the throne of *communion* where Jehovah could righteously and in grace meet His people.

The Shekinah, or cloud of glory, and in itself unapproachable light, out of which Jehovah made Himself known, rested on the Mercy-seat, and was guarded from all unhallowed approach by the Cherubim—the representatives of the Judicial authority of the throne. It was the BLOOD on and before the Mercy-seat which reconciled those two great facts: the majesty of the throne and the presence of a sinful creature in peace before it.

The Tabernacle and the Temple each faced the east, while the Ark and the Mercy-seat stood exactly in front of the beautiful Veil on the west. Thus there was a *direct* line of approach from the Altar without to the Mercy-seat within—from the cross to the throne. "As far as the east (*where stood the Brazen Altar*) is from the west (*the Mercy-seat*), so far hath He removed our transgressions from us" Ps. ciii. 12).

Righteousness is the moral basis of all intercourse between God and man. Grace reigns through righteousness. There is *Divine* righteousness and *human* righteousness. The former is seen in the pure gold of the Mercy-seat; the latter in the tables of the law in the Ark itself. But man is a sinful, an unholy creature, and the law, instead of being obeyed, only convicted him of sin and transgression—he is destitute of goodness and righteousness (Rom. iii.). Now on the proved guilt of man as a law-transgressor the righteousness of God is shewn. The claim of His throne, of His nature, cannot be compromised. Divine righteousness demands Divine judgment. The blood of Christ is the answer to that claim. He has borne the righteous judgment of God against sin. The BLOOD is the great reconciling fact between God in His holiness and man in his sin. The blood on the Mercy-seat proclaims the story of Ps. lxxxv. "Mercy and truth are met together; righteousness and peace have kissed each other" (verse 10). What Christ ever was and is to God in His own Person (the fine gold), that is the measure of His grace to us. The shed and sprinkled blood of Christ was a necessity of the Divine nature if grace to sinners was to have its glorious sway.

THE CHERUBIM.

There were two Cherubim of beaten work of the same piece of gold as the Mercy-seat itself; these were inseparable from, and an integral part of, the Mercy-seat. They were not fastened to it, but were of the *same* piece—part and parcel of the Mercy-seat. There was a Cherub on either end of the Mercy-seat. Both had wings and faces. The wings outspread covered the Mercy-seat, and signified *protecting care* and *rapidity of action.* The faces denoted *intelligence.* The movements of the Cherubim were intelligently directed. They looked to each other, and the gaze of both was set on the blood-sprinkled Mercy-seat. The Cherubim represent the activity of the throne of Jehovah, its Judicial authority. God is said to dwell between the Cherubim (Ps. lxxx. 1; 1 Sam. iv. 4; 2 Kings xix. 15; Isa. xxxvii. 16). The living ones of Rev. iv. and v. are a combination of the Seraphim (Isa. vi.) and the Cherubim (Ezek. i.), and are presented as in and of the throne—an integral, an indispensable part of the throne itself—so with the Cherubim of the Mercy-seat.

The Cherubim set forth that the attributes of God necessarily characterise the action of His throne over all. Those inherent qualities of God—the manifestations of His own character--may be expressed in action through angels or men (see Rev. iv. and v.), but in themselves they simply denote the Judicial authority of the throne. The Lord Jesus Christ carries in Himself the governing authority over all (Matt. xxviii. 18 ; John v. 22, 27).

If the leading passages on the Cherubim are compared and carefully weighed, it must be apparent that they do not signify the Church nor redeemed persons, but simply denote the Judicial authority necessarily connected with the throne of the Eternal in the heavens : Gen. iii. 24 ; Ezek. i., x., xxviii. ; Rev. iv., v.

In Solomon's Temple, in *addition* to the Cherubim on the Mercy-seat, two large ones were built of olive wood and overlaid with gold (1 Kings vi. 23-28). The Cherubim of the Tabernacle looked down upon the propitiatory with satisfaction, for God had been glorified by that blood which had rested on it from one year to another. But the Cherubim of the Temple looked inward or toward the House of Jehovah's rest. All was glorious within, and the Cherubim, the unjealous guardians of the throne, could delight.

> " There were strange soul-depths, restless, vast, and broad,
> Unfathomed as the sea ;
> An infinite craving for some infinite stilling :
> But now Thy perfect love is perfect filling !
> Lord Jesus Christ, my Lord, my God,
> Thou, Thou art enough for me."

The Offerings.

The words sacrifice, oblation, and offering have each their distinctive signification. *Sacrifice* involved the shedding of blood, hence bullocks, lambs, goats, etc., and living animals full of life and free from blemish were killed, as a rule by the offerer, at the north side of the brazen altar (Lev. i. 11); then the officiating priest dealt with the blood in the prescribed manner. *Oblation* referred to the presentation of flour, corn, and the first-fruits of the harvest— that in which there was no blood. *Offering* is a more general word and is applied to both of the foregoing. A bullock for sacrifice and an oblation of fine flour are each termed an offering.

There are four classes of offering: burnt, meat, peace, and sin-offering; these latter include trespass-sacrifices as being alike in character to the sin-sacrifices. These four are referred to in the Epistle to the Hebrews (x. 5-8).

The first official sacrifice offered after the institution of the priesthood is the subject of chapter ix. of Leviticus. On that interesting occasion the glory of Jehovah appeared to the people and fire from before Jehovah consumed the sacrifice. *This* sacred fire was ever to be kept burning. "The fire shall ever be burning upon the altar; it shall never go out." The fire of judgment ever demanded fresh sacrifice, *now* we have a sacrifice which has consumed the fire, and *now* we stand a saved and justified people *in the place where fire has been—the place of the ashes.*

Another point of importance is that the order in which these sacrifices is revealed from God's glory to man's need, or from the burnt-offering to the sin-offering, is not the

order of personal application. In the history of souls the
journey is from self and its need to God, or from the sin-
offering up to the burnt-offering. Thus in Leviticus viii.,
xvi., 2 Chron. xxix., and elsewhere the sin-offerings take
precedence of the burnt-offering.

The revelation of these offerings in the early chapters of
Leviticus is prefaced by the words " the LORD spoke unto
Moses ; " that is, these introductory words intimate a fresh
revelation. Thus the sweet savour offerings (Lev. i.-iii.) having
one character in common are embraced under the prefatory
command in the first verse of the book. The sweet savour
offerings are the burnt-offering, the meat or flour offering,
and the peace or communion offering. The next group of
sacrifices are for the judgment of sin, for positive transgressions committed. In the first class, we have typified—
more or less—the communion of the believer with God, but
here there is no communion ; it is the solemn judgment of
sin. Thus again, " the LORD spake unto Moses " introduces
this new character of sacrifice chapters iv. 1 ; v. 14 ; vi. 1,
8, 19, 24, under this formula distinct revelations from
Jehovah are given.

The fulness of detail and wonderful precision in the com-
munications stamp the Divine record as inspired and
imperishable. Who but God could have foreshown those
shadows of Christ in His Person, life and death. In Christ
those varied gleams and glints centre. *All* have their
answer now in the New Testament Revelation of *one*
Christ, *one* life, *one* sacrifice, *one* mediator, *one* High
Priest.

The Burnt Offering.

LEVITICUS I.

The sacrifices when examined in detail, will be found to yield precious instruction and abundant material for the meditation and worship of the believer.

The burnt offering is the first in Divine order and the highest in character of all the sacrifices. As sinners, we first know Christ as the *trespass* offering "delivered for our offences;" and as led on by the Spirit in the fuller revelation of Christ and His precious sacrifice and Person, we travel upward till we stand as worshippers around the altar of *burnt* offering, and wonder and adore as the ascending flame laden with the divinely-prepared perfume goes up to Jehovah for the satisfaction and rest of His heart. Most blessed it is, however, that God in the order in which these offerings are presented would teach our souls that the self-same sacrifice in which He finds present and eternal delight, is the answer to our need as sinners and our communion as saints. Atonement could be effected by the burnt offering and the various classes of sin offerings, but *not* by either meat or peace offerings.

This sacrifice points to the voluntary surrender, to the free-will offering of Jesus to accomplish *in death* the Divine will, as written of Him in the volume of God's eternal counsels: "Lo, I come to do Thy will, O God" (Heb. x. 7). It is that aspect of the sacrifice of Christ *which* directly and exclusively regards God—"who through the eternal Spirit offered Himself without spot *to God*." In the sin offering there was atonement (chaps. iv., v.) as in the burnt offering; but with this profound difference, that in the former it was

to secure forgiveness—hence the frequent recurrence of the
phrase, "it shall be forgiven him"—while in the burnt
offering it was atonement for the acceptance of the person.
Is it not therefore of priceless value to us that Christ, in the
absolute devotedness of a will wholly set upon His Father's
glory, gave Himself up to God on the altar, and there in the
scene where man had so terribly dishonoured God and
trailed His glory in the dust—yea, in the place of sin-bearing
itself, the fire of Divine judgment was kindled and *all* went
up to God as a sweet savour, and by that *we* are accepted.

The unblemished animal was killed, flayed, and cut in
pieces. The parts enumerated are the "head," the "fat,"
the "inwards," and the "legs"—denoting the *intelligence*,
will, *motives*, and *walk* of the blessed One in thus offering
Himself—a WHOLE Christ and an intelligent surrender to the
glory of God. All were laid upon the altar and subjected
to the fire—the searching judgment of God. "The priest
shall burn *all* upon the altar, to be a burnt sacrifice, an
offering made by fire of a sweet savour unto the LORD."
What the offering was *ceremonially*, being washed in water,
that Jesus was *intrinsically*. The fire of Divine judgment
searched Him inwardly and outwardly; the motives and
springs, as well as the walk and ways—and in result
all went up to God as a sweet savour.

We, through Divine grace and in the power of the Holy
Ghost, identify ourselves with Christ thus so thoroughly
glorifying God—entering into its blessedness, knowing our
acceptance because of His most precious acceptance, and
as thus set down in the holiest of all, in all the value of
Christ's Person and sacrifice. All this is significantly
expressed in the identification of the offerer and the victim:

"And he shall put his hand upon the head of the burnt offering (this significant act only stated in the case of the 'herd,' verse 4), and it shall be accepted for him to make atonement for him." God's eternal delight in Jesus as the burnt offering is beautifully told out in the words: "The fire shall ever be burning upon the altar; it shall never go out" (chap. vi. 13).

The reader's careful attention is called to the distinction between the sweet savour offerings in which the saint is identified in all the Divine acceptance of the sacrifice, and the sin offerings in which the *sinner* is identified in the judgment of the victim.

The Meat Offering.

LEVITICUS II.

This is another of the "sweet savour offerings" in which God's portion and delight in His Son as man are fully brought out. True, in one sense, all that He did, all that He was in life and death was "for us;" but His work to God for the *expiation* of sin is surely a different thing from His work to God for the *acceptance* of the offerer. In the former, God's hatred to sin and outpouring of wrath upon the sinner's substitute is expressed; in the latter, God's delight in holiness and in the infinite perfection of Christ in His Person and death. "Christ made sin for us," characterises the various sin and trespass offerings. Christ giving Himself for us "an offering and a sacrifice to God for a sweet smelling savour," describes the distinguishing feature of the other offerings.

If the burnt offering sets Christ before us coming up to
the altar—the cross—of His own free will, and there, in the
place of sin, and where only it could be expiated, offering
Himself to accomplish the will and glory of God *in death;*
the meat offering presents Him offering a whole unblemished
life to God, and that too, in the place of sin and sorrow.
The material of which it was composed was " fine flour "—
humanity in perfection; its adjuncts were " oil "—the *Holy
Ghost;* " frankincense "—His *moral graces;* and " salt "—
incorruption and *perpetuity.* What was forbidden was
" leaven " (save in *one* marked exception), figure of *evil;*
" honey," type of *mere human affection.* The " oil
poured " upon the offering is the expression of Christ's
anointing by the Spirit and power, as in Acts x. 38 ; while
the offering *mingled* with oil sets forth the profound teaching of Matt. i. 20—" conceived of the Holy Ghost." This
" most holy of the offerings of the LORD made by fire," was
brought to the priests ; a handful taken out with *all* the
frankincense and burnt upon the altar. Thus Christ in all
His blessed life, His words, His ways, His actions, and in
all the moral perfectness and beauties and lovely traits of
that wondrous path, trod to the glory of God, was subjected to the trial of fire. And what was the result? A
sweet savour of rest to God. That part of the offering *not*
put upon the altar, became the food of the priests. Thus
we enjoy communion with God in His expressed delight of
His Beloved One as man on earth. Wondrous privilege !

Neither leaven nor honey was to be burned on the altar
(verse 11). The meat offering of first fruits being baked
with " leaven " (verse 12 ; Lev. xxiii. 17), was an exception,
but this, as setting forth the church at Pentecost, sanctified

and presented to God by the Holy Ghost, could not be "burnt on the altar," for the simple but weighty reason that there was "leaven" or sin there; hence, when the "meat offering," typical of the church, was offered, the loaves made of fine flour were baken with *leaven*, but there was also offered with them a *sin* offering, to meet the actual state of the church, which, of course, on this side of glory is necessarily one of imperfection (Lev. xxiii. 15-21); for the meat offering representing Christ *personally*—in which there was the most careful exclusion of "leaven," see verses 1-10 Lev. ii. The vital connection between the God-glorifying life and death of priceless worth of Jesus, was carefully maintained by an abiding statute when the people were settled in the land, every burnt offering *death* of Jesus), was to be accompanied with a meat offering *life* of Jesus). (Numb. xv. 8-11).

We would again call attention to the interesting and important distinction in these offerings. The four classes of sacrifice were the burnt, meat, peace, and sin offerings, the three former specially expressive of God's delight therein, while the latter expressed His judgment upon sin.

The Peace Offering.

LEVITICUS III.

The essential character of the peace offering being *communion*, a female animal could be offered. In the Church's communion there is necessarily a measure of imperfection and weakness. This seems to be set forth in the "female." But "without blemish" is an indispensable requisite here as in all the sacrifices. God cannot deny Himself. Holiness is an absolute necessity of His nature.

We can readily understand and appreciate surely, in our measure, the appropriate place of this sacrifice as coming after the two already named, the burnt and meat offerings. Our communion in the Person and death of Christ is not only based upon His sacrifice, but partakes of the character of what has already been presented to God, and what He has accepted. Jehovah has already fed upon that which represented Christ in death and life, and according to His delight therein, our souls are maintained in communion. We are thus privileged to feast and joy in common with God, with Christ, and with each other. What an exalted privilege! The portions which Jehovah claimed, here called, "*food* of the offering," were all the "fat" and the "inward parts," that is, the excellency and energy of will, and the feelings, motives, and affections of the Blessed One, which none but God could fully appreciate. All was proved by fire—Divine holiness—everything in Christ was divinely tested, and the trial only brought out His deep perfections. Hence all went up to Jehovah as a sweet savour; yea, more, God fed upon it, found delight and rest in every movement of the heart and will of His Beloved One. In connection with this sacrifice God claimed as a perpetual statute, the "fat" and the "blood," the *will* and *life*.

As nothing, in all connected with the Jewish sacrificial ritual, was left to the imagination of man, but all carefully, minutely, and divinely prescribed, so they, as we, have only to obey, hence the importance of attending to the laws regulating the observance of these sacrifices (chaps. vi., vii.). In this latter chapter we are told what was done with the rest of the animal. The "breast," the *devoted love* of Jesus, was fed upon by Aaron and his sons, typifying Christ and His people. The "right shoulder," the *mighty strength* of Jesus, was the special portion of the priest who offered the blood and burnt the fat. Who could be thus typified save Christ? He is both sacrifice and priest, offerer and victim. The rest of the sacrifice was eaten on the day or day after it was offered by the offerer and his friends. On the third day whatever remained must be burnt on the altar, setting forth the weighty truth that *communion* cannot be prolonged beyond the measure of one's spiritual power and capacity. Working oneself into fellowship with God, or the fleshly effort to maintain communion, is most certainly an abomination to the Lord (verse 18, chap. vii.). The peace offering presents a truly wonderful sight: God, Christ, the Christian, and the Church together feeding— together delighting in Jesus, and in His love, Person, and sacrifice.

Precious Saviour, Thou joy of our hearts, Thou infinitely Blessed One, maintain our communion uninterrupted until we see Thee face to face.

The Sin Offering.

LEVITICUS IV.

The various sin offerings being identified with that which was in itself abhorrent to God, were not burnt on the altar, but were either wholly consumed "outside the camp," God thus marking His sense of the terrible character of sin, even when laid on Jesus—His soul's delight—Who "suffered without the gate," saying, as the expression of His soul's agony in that awful hour, "My God, My God, why hast Thou forsaken Me?"—or eaten by the priests in the Court (vi. 26). But let it ever be remembered, that even in those sacrifices which represented Christ made sin for us, and thus *only* on the cross made *officially* obnoxious to God, yet *personally* He never was more dear to His God and Father; for the blood (the *life*) was sprinkled before Jehovah, and in certain cases put upon the horns of the golden altar—*worship;* and upon the brazen altar—*approach;* while *all* the fat was burnt upon the altar, ascending to Jehovah and heaven as a sweet savour.

The various grades in the offering shew God taking into account the poverty of His people (Luke ii. 24), and they may also express the various measures of apprehension found amongst God's people in respect to the one sacrifice of Christ. If we have *measures* of apprehension, we have also *degrees* of sin, and this latter is specially pointed out here. The gravity of sin must be measured by the dignity of the offended One, and the relative position of the offender. First, then, we have the sin of the anointed priest (chap. iv. 3-12); secondly, of the whole congregation (13-21): thirdly, of the ruler (22-26); fourthly, of any of the common people (27-35). If the priest who represented the people before Jehovah, or the congregation sinned, the blood—the witness of death—was sprinkled seven times (*spiritual perfection*) before the Lord, and also put upon the horns of the golden altar. This latter use of the blood was in order that the worship and communion of the redeemed congregation might be righteously and holily maintained, or, if lost, restored; but when a prince or ruler, or one of the common people transgressed, the worship of the Lord's host was not necessarily interrupted, and hence, in their case, the blood was merely put upon the horns of the brazen altar. The sin of the anointed priest, and the corporate sin of the whole congregation, were the most serious cases of any ; on their sin the judgment of God rested more heavily than in the other cases, for in theirs only is it said that the sin offering was to be wholly burned outside the camp. It may be remarked, that so thoroughly is this aspect of the death of Jesus identified with the sin of man, that in the original it is the same word for " sin " and " sin offering."

All these sacrifices and the teachings based thereon, have a solemn voice to us, and teach us deeply impressive lessons, which may God grave upon our heart.

The Trespass Offering.

LEVITICUS v., vi. 7.

The distinction between sin and trespass may here be pointed out. Trespass refers to *acts* done against God or man, sin to the *root* from whence these acts proceed. It will be observed that in the sin offerings, particular acts are not specified, as the immediate object is the condemnation of sins, and the man is regarded as a *sinner*, but in the various trespass offerings, particular offences are carefully enumerated, and the man regarded as a *transgressor*. All transgression is sin, but all sin does not necessarily partake of the character of transgression. In the sin offerings the victim and the offerer are identified, the laying on of hands on the head of the victim being the fit expression of this identity; but this was never done in cases of trespass, although confession, full and ample, was required. Thus in the sin offerings the *condemnation* of sin is the great point, while in the trespass offerings the *confession* of sin is a necessity.

It is of profound importance to note carefully that sin is not measured by conscience or knowledge of what is evil, but by the holiness of God. Thus sins of ignorance were not excusable or passed lightly over, but had to be provided for in the most solemn manner possible (chap. iv.).

In the trespass offerings, to meet offences done *against the Lord*, whether known or unknown, the blood of a victim alone could suffice, besides the offender making ample amends for the harm done. In the first thirteen verses of chapter v. the prescribed ritual is to meet sin and trespass together.

In cases of trespass against one's neighbour, restitution for the wrong done must be full and ample, the principal had to be restored and a fifth part added. This would satisfy man's claim, but even in these cases, forgiveness and atonement, as always, can only be obtained through the death of another, "for without shedding of blood is no remission." After these sacrifices had been duly instituted, and the laws regulating their due observance been established, the consecration of the priesthood naturally follows, which we do not enter upon here. Sacrifice necessarily precedes priesthood; yea, more, is the basis of all true acceptable worship, and the ground of the priestly grace of our Great High Priest.

Wilderness Defilement;

OR, THE RED HEIFER.

NUMBERS XIX.

This was a special provision to meet wilderness defilement. Our standing as Christians before God is founded on the accomplished work of the cross (Lev. xvi.). Our whole condition as sinners has been divinely met, and that for God and eternity, by the blood of Christ. Our weakness, infirmity, and sorrow as saints have their blessed answer in the unchangeable priesthood of the Son of God on high; while positive failure and defilement, contracted while passing on to our eternal rest, are securely provisioned for in the advocacy of Christ with the Father, in answer to which the Spirit brings the written Word (the *running water*, Num. xix.) and the rememberance of Christ in agony and death (the *ashes*, Num. xix.) to bear upon the conscience of the erring one. Confession full and thorough follows, and the result is that the impaired communion with God is again restored. But be it carefully noted that this is Divine provision for a saint of God, one whose standing is in Divine righteousness, and of whose eternal safety there is not the least doubt.

The red heifer must be spotless, unblemished, "*wherein is no blemish,*" and "*upon* which never came yoke." Thus is Christ set forth in absolute perfection of His *nature*, and in the holiness of His *life*. Like the sin offering, whose blood was taken *inside*, the animal was wholly consumed outside the camp, but with this marked peculiarity that the fat and the blood—the *excellency* and the *life*—were also consumed, save a little of the blood, which was reserved,

and sprinkled *seven* times (*perfection*) before the door of the
Tabernacle—the meeting place between Jehovah and His
people.   Thus the witness of death was brought before the
eye of God.   Cedar wood, hyssop, and scarlet were then
cast into the midst of the burning.   Human nature in its
best estate (*cedar*), in its lowest form (*hyssop*), and all
earthly glory (*scarlet*) for the Christian, went in the cross of
Christ.   The ashes—remembrance of Christ's agony and
wrath of God—were carefully gathered up as a " purification
for sin, " and along with running water—figure of the
searching and convicting Word of God—were sprinkled by
a clean person on the defiled one, on the third and seventh
days.   The third day's sprinkling was in view of *his sin,*
the second sprinkling was in light of *God's grace.*   The
first would lead to a deepening sense of what sin is in light
of what Christ suffered, and the other application of the
ashes and water would as surely lead to a more profound
sense of what grace can accomplish as the fruit of the cross.

Blessed Saviour, we shall soon be with Thee, and our
sinning and suffering be all over.

The Day of Atonement.

LEVITICUS XVI.

The word "Atonement"—the very embodiment of fundamental truth—does not occur in the original New Testament
Scriptures.   It is found once in the Authorised English
Version of Rom. v. 11, the margin of which, however,
rightly reads " reconciliation."   But although the word
does not occur in the New Testament, yet the precious

truth, as a whole, and in all its parts, is unfolded therein. We may here remark that the result of Jewish sacrifice was to *cover* sin from God's sight (Ps. xxxii. 1); the result of the sacrifice of Christ is to put it away completely and eternally (Heb. ix. 26). We must turn to the pages of the Old Testament where alone the word is used, for a scriptural answer to the oft-repeated question, "What is Atonement?"

A reference to a good concordance will show that "Atonement" occurs about thirty times in the book of Leviticus—half of its verbal biblical references. Why is this? Because Atonement not only necessitates a sacrifice, but a sanctuary, and also a high priest to deal with the sacrificial blood. Now these—*i.e.*, a sacrifice, a sanctuary, and priest—are prominent features of the third book of Scripture, especially of chap. xvi., where the verb to make Atonement, *i.e.* to *cover* (the noun is not met with in the chapter), occurs no less than fifteen times—a chapter which unfolds in type the whole work of Atonement, both in its essential elements, as also in its varied and interesting details. Both Redemption and Atonement for us are by blood, but unlike the former, the latter requires the service of the High Priest to deal with the blood in the holiest. Redemption is not dependent on the ministry of the priest, nor on the value of the Sanctuary. Atonement is first met with in Gen. vi. 14, *pitched* or *covered*. The ark was made judgment-proof without and within—for sins committed and for sin, *i.e.* the nature.

The ritual observed on the annual day of Atonement was both impressive and suggestive (Lev. xvi.). It was the only day of the year when the duties of the ordinary priests were suspended in the Sanctuary (verse 17), for they also, as all the people, needed Atonement to be made for all their sins (verses 33, 34). It was also a day of entire cessation from all work—this was imperative upon all Israelites, and strangers amongst them (verses 29-31)—the only occasion, moreover, when the high priest laid aside h s pontifical attire "for glory and for beauty," and arrayed himself in linen garments. Both sets of garments are termed "holy garments" (Exod. xxviii. 2 ; Lev. xvi. 4).

There are several main elements in the scriptural teaching of Atonement. It might be well to compare current theological teaching with God's answer to the question, What is Atonement? *First*, we have God's judgment upon, and death of the sacrificial animals (Lev. xvi., 24, 6, 9). *Second*, sprinkling of the blood by the high priest in the Sanctuary, once upon the Mercy-seat and seven times before it. This important action could only be performed by the High Priest of the nation (verse 14). *Third*, the confession of the sins of the people. Putting all the confessed sins upon the head of the scapegoat, or "goat of departure," and its dismissal into a land of separation (verse 21, 22). This, too, could only be done by Aaron as representing the nation before God. Azazel, or "goat of departure," occurs but four times in the Word and only in this chapter. These and other features combined constitute Atonement.

These various elements of Atonement are separately treated of in the New Testament, although the word which expresses the whole is not there used. Many expressions in common use really narrow the scope of the comprehensive and fundamental truth of Atonement.

Propitiation.

Atonement is a word found only in the earlier Revelation —the Old Testament. Propitiation occurs alone in the later volume of Inspiration—the New Testament. On the tenth day of the seventh month, the high priest, clad in garments of white, annually entered the Sanctuary, not without blood —the solemn witness of death (Lev. xvi.). Atonement, typically as a whole, and, of course, in all its parts, had to be effected on that one day of twenty-four hours. No part of it could be left over till the following day. What was said of Boaz of old might have been said of Aaron, Israel's first high priest on the Atonement-day, and surely more so of Christ in view of effecting Atonement—once and for ever: "The man will not be in rest, until he hath finished the thing this day."

Now *Propitiation* and *Substitution* were essential parts of Atonement. The former was solely the work of the high priest, as he alone could enter the innermost part of the Sanctuary to sprinkle the atoning blood on the Mercy-seat and before it; the latter, too, was the work of the high priest, but as the nation's representative before God. He alone could make Propitiation, and this he did by blood: sprinkling the blood once upon the Mercy-seat—Jehovah's throne in the midst of a sinful and guilty people— also seven times before the Mercy-seat or Propitiatory (v. 14). Propitiation is thus towards God, as Substitution is towards believers. The blood on the Mercy-seat made *Propitiation*. Our sins borne by Christ is *Substitution*. Now, Propitiation, it will be observed, was effected by blood-*sprinkling*—that is the presentation of the blood God-ward; not simply by

blood-*shedding*.   *Shed* at the altar, *sprinkled* on and before
the Mercy-seat.   The latter was the work of the priest; the
former generally that of the offerer beside the altar.   Christ
as High Priest, and in the upper Sanctuary, has made
Propitiation by His own blood (compare Lev. xvi. 14-17 the
type, with Heb. ix. 11, 12 the antitype).   This He alone
could do in His character and office as a merciful and
faithful High Priest (Heb. ii. 17, where "reconciliation"
should read "propitiation").   But He has not only made
it by His blood, but He *is* now the Propitiation, or, blood-
sprinkled-Mercy-seat (1 John ii. 2 ;   iv. 10;   Rom. iii. 25).
It will be observed that Propitiation is always for sins and
uncleanness of every description and character (Lev. xvi.
16).   "He is the propitiation for *our sins*" 1 John ii. 2),
i.e., for those of believers only, and for, or on behalf of, the
whole world.

Propitiation is the satisfying of God's claims in respect
to His nature.   The blood of the Substitute could alone
accomplish this, and Christ as High Priest was alone
competent to do it, and only in the heavenly Sanctuary, *i.e.*,
the immediate presence of God.   He shed His blood as a
victim; by it He entered into the holiest as High Priest
(Heb. ix. 12).   Carefully distinguish between the blood
shed and *sprinkled*.   This latter effects propitiation.

Substitution.

"We died *in* the person of our Substitute" is an unscriptural expression.   The word does not say "we died in Christ,"
else we must have shared in God's judgment on Christ on
the cross.   Because we are *in Christ*, in contrast to our

being *in Adam*, we consequently share in the blessed consequences flowing from such a connection. The condition of the Head of the race determines that of each member of it. Hence it is equally true of us, as of Him, that we are:—

Dead with Him to sin, to the law, etc., (Rom. vi ; vii.).

Quickened with Him (Eph. ii. 5).

Risen with Him (Col. iii. 1).

Seated in Him in heavenly places (Eph. ii. 6).

We never get "*in* Him" till Ascension is viewed. It will be of great advantage to Bible students to note the truth in its order and exactness. "Accepted in the sacrifice," is not the truth of Lev. i. There we read, "it (the sacrifice) shall be accepted for him" (verse 4); not we accepted *in* it, but just the reverse—"*it for him.*" The phrase "accepted in the beloved," as in our ordinary version, is a misleading thought, Eph. i. 6 R.V. conveying a totally different line of idea from acceptance in Christ.

This term, "Substitution," nowhere occurs in Scripture, but the truth of which the word is the expression is taught in both Testaments. Dying for our sins (1 Cor. xv. 3), and bearing our sins (1 Peter ii. 24) are exclusively believers' truths, and substitutionary in character. Universal bearing of sins involves the unscriptural thought of universal salvation. Both are utterly false.

Substitution is *one instead of another* not "one *in* another." It is the actual bearing of the sins of all who believe—only of such (1 Peter ii. 24 ; Isa. liii. 6). We may remark that we are neither directed to "look on the blood," nor to "lay our sins on Jesus." We could do neither. Jehovah has done both. "When *I* see the blood I will pass over you " (Exod. xii. 13), and " *Jehovah* hath laid on Him the iniquity of us all " (Isa. liii. 6).

Our souls rest on God's mighty delivering work : our confidence is in what He has done and said, as to *that*. Evangelists and teachers should be extremely careful and guarded in their statements on this vital truth. Loose and careless remarks on this subject have wrought an incalculable amount of mischief to souls. It is not said in the Scriptures that Christ bore the sins of the world. He tasted death for all (Heb. ii. 9), but bore only the sins of His own. This latter, we repeat, was substitutionary. "The *sin* of the world " (John i. 29), and " Christ was once offered to bear the *sins* of many " (Heb. ix. 28)—*i.e.*, of believers— are accurately distinguished in Scripture. The confession of Israel's sins over the scapegoat and its dismissal never to re-appear, finely illustrate the truth of Substitution (Lev. xvi. 21-22).

Preach Propitiation to sinners—the blood on the Mercy-seat, and God in righteousness and grace freely receiving all who will but come. *Teach* Substitution to believers— their sins confessed and borne by Christ, and never to be remembered.

The Priesthood of Christ and of Believers.

First, as to the priesthood of the blessed Lord : It is an integral part of Christianity, as the Aaronic priesthood was of the Levitical system. The Lord's present priestly service is founded on God's acceptance of the sacrifice, and is exercised alone on behalf of those who are saved. The

SPHERE of His priesthood is heaven. He could not be a priest on earth (Heb. viii. 4), says the apostle. The earthly Sanctuary could only be entered by the sons of Levi, while Christ as to earthly descent came from the royal tribe—Judah, "of which tribe Moses spake nothing concerning priesthood," and "of which no man gave attendance at the altar" (Heb. vii. 11-14). Connect *royalty* with Judah, and *priesthood* with Levi.

The ORDER of the Lord's priesthood is after that of Melchisedec (Heb. v. 6)—type of the Lord in the glory and dignity of his Person (vii. 1-3). Thus there is secured for us an "unchangeable priesthood." What strength this imparts to tried and suffering saints! (verse 25). The Melchisedec character of priesthood is millennial, and will be exercised by the Lord when "He shall be a priest upon His throne" (Zech. vi. 13)—a combination of royal authority and priestly grace.

The PATTERN of the Lord's priesthood is after that of Aaron's—type of the Lord's in present priestly grace. It is threefold in character—*first*, making propitiation by blood in the holiest as did Aaron (Lev. xvi. 14; Heb. ii. 17; ix. 11, 12). The blood was *shed* at the altar outside; it was then carried in by the high priest and *sprinkled* on and before the throne inside. This latter is termed "propitiation." It has been done once, and in its nature is incapable of repetition; *second*, succouring the tempted, sympathising with infirmity, and supplying mercy and grace in time of need (Heb. ii. 18; iv. 14-16); *third*, in practically maintaining us all along the way—ever living to intercede for us—saving even to the "uttermost" of human need – taking account of our sorrows, difficulties,

trials, exercises, and tears (vii. 25). His compassion and
tenderness are boundless. He leads our worship, and in
all things, and at all times represents us before God in the
heavenly Sanctuary. His own special place there is on
" the right hand of the throne of the Majesty." There He
sits as our " *Great* High Priest "—a title of dignity peculiar
to our Lord. The Priesthood of Christ is not to procure
righteousness, but to help, bless, comfort, and sustain a
people made righteous through grace. The priesthood is
only exercised on behalf of believers.

Second, as to the priesthood of believers. All true
Christians are priests to God (Rev. i. 5, 6); all having an
equal title to draw near (Heb. x. 22). The *Jewish* priest
and the *Christian* priest have each their sacrifice, sanctuary,
and guide-book as to worship. Leviticus was the guide-book
of the Jewish worshipper : while 1 Cor. xi.-xiv. and
Hebrews form the guide and directory to the Christian
worshipper. Our sacrifices as priests, are praise to *God*—
the fruit of lips touched by the live coal of judgment—and
practical benevolence *to man* (Heb. xiii. 15, 16). The
former is referred to by Peter when he styles us a "*holy*
priesthood;" and the latter, when he regards us as a "*royal*
priesthood" (1 Pet. ii. 5-9). It is interesting to observe,
that when the priesthood of all believers is directly referred
to, the high priesthood of our Lord is not mentioned at all, as
in 1 Peter and the Revelation. Judaism sent the worshipper
of old to the priest; Christianity reveals direct approach to
God by Him, *i.e.*, the ever-living priest. The priests of old
stood outside the holiest. The veil was unrent and the
conscience unpurged. The priests of Christian times stand
and worship inside the holiest; the veil is rent and the

conscience purged. The former could never enter the holiest. The latter enter the holiest: the blood their title. Priestly functions are not confined to a favoured class. *All* believers are priests, irrespective of age, maturity in divine life, or attainments in either the intellectual or spiritual domains. In ministry there are distinctions. In worship there is none.

Priesthood and ministry are totally distinct truths: the former is towards *God*; the latter towards *man*.

Synoptical View of the Offerings.

1.—Lev. i.

THE BURNT OFFERING.

MATERIAL.

Bullocks, goats, sheep, rams, lambs, turtle-doves, and young pigeons.

SIGNIFICATION.

Christ's absolute devotedness and voluntary surrender of Himself in *death* to accomplish the will and glory of God. It is that aspect of the cross which exclusively regards God, while of infinite value to us (Heb. ix. 14; John x. 17, 18).

NOTES.

This was the first in order, and the highest in character of all the sacrifices.

The acceptance of the offerer, according to the value of the sacrifice of Christ to God, is characteristic of this offering.

The offerer, as identified with the acceptance of the victim, also identifies himself with its death and ceremonial purity (verses 3-6); so we are accepted in *His* acceptance, entering also into the reality of His death and His absolute purity.

On special occasions the trumpets were blown over these offerings as a memorial before God (Num. x. 10).

When in the land the *burnt* and *flour* offerings were ever to be associated, for God would ever have the *death* and *life* of His Son thus prefigured before Him.

2.—Lev. ii.

THE FLOUR OFFERING.

MATERIAL.

"Fine flour" or bruised corn; its adjuncts were oil, frankincense, and salt.

SIGNIFICATION.

Christ as man meeting perfectly the Father's will, and perfectly accomplishing the Father's glory in a *life* most holy, and where every moral grace and beauty of heart and life were displayed before God and man. It is alone as *priests* that our souls feed upon, and worship *Him* Who tabernacled amongst us.

NOTES.

The "fine flour" sets forth the holy humanity of our Lord. *Mingled* with the oil refers to the conception of our Lord by the Holy Ghost (Matt. i. 20); while the flour *anointed* with the oil would express the weighty truth conveyed in Acts x. 38.

God's part of this offering was a handful of flour with the oil, and " *all* the frankincense ; " for God alone could fully appreciate the moral glories and perfections of Christ's Person and ways.

This offering, and the sin-sacrifices, are termed "*most holy.*" Laid on the brazen altar, it was thus based upon, and its value declared by, what God found in the death of Jesus.

Neither honey (mere human sweetness) nor leaven (evil) was to be offered, save in one notable instance as to the introduction of the latter, but then the Church and not Christ is in view (Lev. xxiii. 17).

3.—Lev. iii.

THE COMMUNION OFFERING.
MATERIAL.

Bullocks, lambs, and goats,—male or female.

SIGNIFICATION.

Christ, in the perfection and value of His sacrifice, the ground, measure, and material of our individual and Church communion with God. What deep, rich, and blessed soul-enjoyments are ours! God, Christ, and the priestly family feed, feast, and rejoice together.

NOTES.

This offering was expressive of the *communion* of saints, and not the making of peace for the sinner.

The fat *(energy)*, inwards *(affections)*, and blood *(life)*, were the parts claimed by God as a sweet savour, and on which He could feed and find satisfaction.

The breast *(love)*, and the shoulder *(strength)*, were eaten by Aaron, his sons, and the males of the children of Israel. The remainder of the animal, if any left, was burnt on the third day, as communion with God can only be maintained in connection with the sacrifice.

Both this and the flour-offering, being laid on the altar of burnt-offering, derived their worth and value from what God found in the blessed self-surrender of Jesus to accomplish the will and glory of God.

In this chapter, God's part, termed "*food* of the offering," is given, while in chapter vii. our part is detailed.

4.—Lev. iv.
THE SIN OFFERING.
MATERIAL.

Bullocks, rams, goats and their young, lambs, pigeons, and turtle-doves. The tenth part of an ephah of fine flour was an exceptional sin-offering.

SIGNIFICATION.

Christ most holy, yet made sin for us. As the great sin-offering He cried, "My God, My God, why hast Thou forsaken Me?" Christ identified with our guilt and expiating our sin under the judgment of God.

NOTES.

The goat was specially the sin-offering, hence the wicked are so termed (Matt. xxv. 33).

The sin-offerings, as also the flour-offerings, were termed "*most holy.*"

The sin-sacrifices were not sweet savour offerings; charged with sin, they could not be so regarded, nor were they offered for the acceptance of the person or his communion with God, but for the expiation of sin. "It shall be forgiven him" is the characteristic truth.

The offerings varied according to the position of the offender, but sin was measured not by conscience but by the character of God.

The fat *(excellency)* could alone be burned on the altar, and ascend to God as a sweet savour.

5.—Lev. v.

THE TRESPASS OFFERING.

MATERIAL.

Rams, and he-lambs.

SIGNIFICATION.

Christ's most holy sacrifice of Himself for our sins—of His shed blood—the alone ground of forgiveness; and restitution for wrong committed—whether against God or man—an imperative necessity.

NOTES.

In these offerings, the individual *acts* are specially in view.

In the *sin*-offering, the person's guilt before God is the main thought, here it is in reference to the injury one has done.

Hands were laid on the burnt-offering, thus identifying the person with its acceptance; in the sin-offering, hands were also laid, but there it was identified with the person's guilt; here, however, no hands were laid on the animal.

Sacrifice, restitution, with an additional part added—a fifth as interest, accompanied by confession, were essential to a full forgiveness.

Most of the particulars bearing upon the *sin*-offerings, are equally applicable to the *trespass*-offerings.

6.—Num. xv.

THE DRINK OFFERING.

MATERIAL.

"Strong wine poured unto the Lord" (Num. xxviii. 7).

SIGNIFICATION.

Christ, in His unblemished life and voluntary death, affording joy to God and man—the joy in proportion to the value of what was typified in the flour (*life*) and burnt offerings (*death*) (Judges ix. 13).

NOTES.

The first mention of a drink-offering is in Gen. xxxv. 14.

After the formal institution of the Levitical system, drink-offerings were to be poured out only in connection with the burnt and flour-offerings, that is, as expressive of the joy which the life *(flour)* and death *(burnt)* of Jesus impart.

The quantity of wine varied according to the value of the animal, but the quantity of wine and oil always corresponded, for joy in Christ is always according to the power of the Holy Ghost—the oil.

Drink-offerings will again be poured out before the Lord, as the expression of millennial gladness.

"Yea, and if I be *poured out* as a libation on the sacrifice and ministration of your faith, I joy and rejoice with you all" (Phil. ii. 17). Thus Paul presents himself as a sacrificial drink-offering.

Nos. 1, 2, 3 were sweet savour offerings, expressive of Jehovah's delight in Christ, and were also specially connected with the acceptance and communion of the worshipper ; on the contrary, nos. 4, 5 intimated God's solemn judgment upon sin, and thus the forgiveness of the sinner is the prominent thought ; while no. 6 tells of God's joy, and man's too, in the life and death of Jesus.

The special ordinances of the red heifer to meet wilderness defilement (Num. xix.), and of the Passover, commemorative of deliverance from judgment (Exod. xii.), as also of the annual atonement (Lev. xvi.), are exceptions to these sacrifices and the laws which govern them. Salt (*incorruption*) was not to be omitted from any of the sacrifices ; it is specially named in connection with the flour-offering (*life of Jesus*). "Azazel," meaning *goat of departure*, occurs four times, and only in Lev. xvi.

MEDITATION AT THE LORD'S SUPPER.

Agony of agony !
Oh, listen to that awful cry
Piercing through mysterious night
When cloudless sun gives out no light !
Hark ! It beats 'gainst black-brass sky—
"Eli lama sabachthani !"

Agony of agony !
What the pain of Calvary ?
Not the mocking taunt nor blow,
Not the thorn that tears the brow,
Not the great indignity
Of sinners striking Deity ;—
Not the rod that furrows plowed,
Not the ribald soldier-crowd,
Blinding first, then even hitting—
The vilest on His features spitting
(Jew as well as Gentile spitting)
On that Face so greatly scarred,
Soon by deeper sorrow marred.
'Twas not these that forced the cry,
"Eli lama sabachthani !"

Agony of agony !
What the pain of Calvary ?
Never moan nor grief-fraught wail
Follows the nerve-tearing nail—
True He speaks—He is but pleading—
For His slayers interceding.
Meekest Lamb to slaughter come !
Sheep before her shearers dumb !
'Tis not shame His spirit grieves
As He hangs betwixt the thieves ;
Not the gibe of passer-by,
Nor more cruel priests that cry
"Saviour He of others—save
'Self He cannot from the grave."

Even not the cruel smart
Added to that gentle Heart,
When He with true human pain
Looks for pity—looks in vain.
It needs still deeper agony
E'en than these to wake the cry
" Eli lama sabachthani."

Agony of agony !
This the pain of Calvary :
Bow, my soul, in solemn awe,
From thy foot the sandal draw :
This is truly holy ground,
Here is mystery profound.
Few thy words—but let thy thought
Be with deep emotion fraught :
Tremble whilst Truth speaks to Guilt,
Telling why that blood was spilt ;
Weep e'en whilst sweet Mercy's voice
Bids thy broken heart rejoice ;
Praise, whilst Love and Truth unite,
Flooding heart with heavenly light,—
Trembling, weeping, praising, learn
(*Let it in thy spirit burn*)
Thy sins—thyself hast caused that cry—
" *Eli lama sabachthani !* "

(Pause—nor shame if 'scape a sigh,
   Or a tear thine eye bedews.
Melting soul, and brimming eye
   Fit the scene on which ye muse.
Sighing here speaks not of grief ;
Gentle tears are love's relief.

Yea, for since I've learnt *my* part,
   In that solemn scene I ponder,
Mem'ries of a broken heart
   Tenderly must linger yonder.
Whilst, to make such visions clear,
No lens like a contrite tear.)

But e'en whilst the city walls
　　Those sad echoes back are flinging,
Golden sunlight once more falls ;
　　And the birds resume their singing.
That dread storm is past forever—
Past ! to be repeated —*never !*

List ！　His voice again is heard,
　　In the calm of conqueror, sending
Forth His spirit with a word,
　　To His Father all commending ;—
Speaks, but with no breath of sighing—
Dies, but with no sign of dying !

Thus He's numbered with the dead,
　　For by man no bone is broken.
God alone may bruise *this* " Bread "—
　　Man may loose love's mightiest token—
One last blow—the soldier's spear
Fills our cup with " Wine to cheer."

Nevermore shall unbelief
　　Put its cruel mark upon Him ;
Nevermore shall pain or grief
　　Leave their scarring traces on Him.
Henceforth love alone shall pour
On His feet her richest store,

Sing, ye angels !　ye whose eyes
　　Long to scan redemption's story ;
See your own Creator rise,—
　　But now robed in other glory—
Hail your Lord your God again
" As a Lamb that hath been slain ! "

Sing, ye saints, who know the bliss
　　Of that word " Thou art forgiven "—
Know the rapture of God's kiss ;
　　Be *ye* not outpraised by heaven !
Which, think ye, should love Him most,
　　Sinners saved, or angel host ?

"Sing, my soul!"   each saved one cries,
  As we sit around His table,
"Mine the song whose note shall rise
  High o'er all.   If I were able;
Saint and angel I'd outvie,
None can *owe* so much as I.

"Though my fullest song is faint—
Though my fire's but smould'ring ember—
Though my praise oft turns to plaint—
  Lord, I can at least '*remember*.'
This I do as now we sup—
Break the bread and drink the cup."

By kind permission of the writer—F. C. J.

"BY ONE OFFERING

HE HATH PERFECTED

FOR EVER

THEM THAT ARE SANCTIFIED"

(Heb. x. 14).